Another Man's Shoes

Sven Sømme

with an Introduction by

Ellie Sømme

D0542271

© Ellie Targett 2005

ISBN 978-0954913731

Second edition 2011

Published by
Polperro Heritage Press
Clifton-upon-Teme
Worcestershire WR6 6EN
United Kingdom
polperro.press@virgin.net

Cover design by Orphans Press

Printed in Great Britain by
Orphans Press
Arrow Close, Enterprise Park,
Leominster, Herefordshire
HR6 0LD

Foreword

Another Man's Shoes vividly captures the atmosphere of life in occupied Norway during WW2. Lovers of nature and the free outdoors life, Norwegians were never going to be willingly oppressed. In this moving account of the courage, determination and self-sacrifice exhibited by the Norwegian resistance movement, I found a timely reminder of how important it remains to oppose tyranny and dictatorship.

Ray Mears

*This book is dedicated to the men and women of Norway
who fought for the freedom of their country.*

Acknowledgments

To Corinne Souza, author of *Baghdad Spy* for her support and encouragement; to Linda Cracknell, writer and mountain goat, for her courage and fortitude; to my brother Bertie, son Oliver and sister Yuli, my dearest companion to the end. To our cousin Sven for help in the planning of our route retracing Pappa's footsteps; to Oddmund who showed us the way and to all our new friends in Norway who were so welcoming and helpful. To Mum for her memories; my husband Keith for his patience and love, and to our son Sven who bears Pappa's name. To Mike Dickins for his belief in the story; to Anne and Paddy Beresford who were the first to read it; to Jan Tystad for the translation and for bringing the story to the Norwegian public's attention; to Ray Mears for his interest, and to Lauritz for his unstinting support and help in planning the route and for giving us Iacob's speech.

CONTENTS

Introduction

The wave of emotion hit me and for a moment I held back. Then I let the tears fall.

"Pappa's shoes," I whispered.

As the room fell silent I looked at Selma, standing in front of me. "Pappa's shoes," I whispered again. In her sunlit sitting room with our new-found friends and the waiting journalists gathered around I hugged her. This courageous old lady had kept the shoes for over 60 years, worn and with the laces still tied they bound us together; they had even survived the fire which engulfed her home ten years earlier and which was still too difficult for her to talk about. They were the shoes Pappa wore when the German commandant had said: "You'll be shot for this, you know that don't you, you'll certainly be shot." The shoes he wore when he was handcuffed and marched with an armed guard through his home town of Molde. The shoes he wore when he escaped from the ship and walked past the armed German guards with a friendly wave. And the same shoes he had worn when he made his way through the snow to the small community of Isfjorden where a young girl and her friends had risked their own lives to offer him help.

"You can't go into the mountains in those shoes," Selma's brother-in-law Henry Berg had said to my father. "I have a new pair of mountain boots, we can swap."

Selma had said in her letter to me three weeks earlier: 'I have a present for you'. And here I was with my sister Yuli, brother Bert, my son Oliver and Yuli's friend Linda with Selma and her family and the waiting journalists.

Selma gave a little talk while we ate the cakes and drank the coffee she had prepared. She spoke of her work in the Norwegian resistance during the war and of the help they had given to escapees trying to reach Sweden, my father being one of them. And with her voice breaking with emotion she told us about the fire that had destroyed her home. Then she crossed to the old piano standing in a corner and, giving herself a note, she sang a hymn to us, in her still strong, beautiful voice. We listened in silence, and then she said: "I have a present for you".

*

To my shame, I didn't read my father's account of his escape until nearly 20 years after his death from cancer in 1961. I was busy with my family and work and there was always another book to finish reading first. Mum had mentioned it a few times and it was one of those things 'I must do'. And so time had gone on, and I remember when I first picked it up I read as far as his arrest and then it took me another six months before I could finish it. Silly really. I knew he had survived, I was born long after the war but somehow I feared for him even though I knew. I grew up with the story, knew that my father was a hero (aren't all fathers?) but like all small children I was busy with friends and with school.

We lived on the West coast of Norway just outside the small market town of Molde where my father had also grown up. His father had been the local doctor who ran the hospital from 1920. Pappa was the youngest of five: Ingrid, Iacob, Knud, Helene and him, Sven. When he was born in 1904 his family lived close to the town of Lillehammer in the eastern part of Norway. His father, Iacob Dybwad Somme (1866-1923) was one of the founding physicians at the Mesnalien Sanatorium for the treatment of tuberculosis. The fresh forest air of the area was part of the cure. Patients took daily walks in the forest, or spent several hours on the terrace every day, even when the temperature fell below zero and they had to be covered in sheepskin blankets. The sanatorium was known for its high quality and comfort. According to Dr. Sømme, nobody should reduce their standard of living because they were unlucky enough to get tuberculosis.

Of the five brothers and sisters, Iacob was perhaps the most involved with the Norwegian resistance during the Second World War. As head of intelligence for Milorg, the military organization of the resistance movement, he developed methods for espionage, and had important messages sent by radio to Britain or by courier to Sweden. He was arrested in October of 1942 and spent nearly 18 months in prison. His New Year's Eve speech to his fellow prisoners on the 31st December 1943 became famous [see Iacob's Story]. It was full of hope for the nation's future freedom but, tragically, he was taken out with six other prisoners on the 2nd March and shot in reprisal for the bombing of the heavy water by the resistance at Rykan.

Sven's sister Ingrid was also engaged in resistance work during the war, but had to leave for Sweden in 1942. In Gothenburg she was active in organizing the so-called Norway aid. Large quantities of food were sent to Norway as a supplement to the strict rationing enforced by the Germans. She also collected and sent supplies for the Norwegian resistance movement through secret ship passages.

Sven's eldest brother, Knud, was a civil engineer and spent most of his career working in paper mills and cellulose factories. During the war he too was involved with the resistance and played an important role in helping Sven escape in 1944. As a result he received a warning from the resistance that he may be wanted by the Germans; he knew too much and would be subjected to torture if he was arrested. He and his family were 'invited' to flee and subsequently met up with Sven at the refugee camp in Sweden in August of that year.

Although Sven's youngest sister, Helene, did not participate in the resistance movement, she supported Ingrid and her three brothers in their work. They would often meet at her house, which on some occasions also served as a refuge for people on the run from the Gestapo.

*

A typical Norwegian, my father Sven loved the mountains and the fjords and would spend his holidays skiing, swimming, fishing and hunting and studying the wildlife. He became a marine biologist, just like his elder brother, Iacob, and travelled to England in the early 1920's to study. There he met my English mother, Primrose Tozer. She was just seven and he was a young man of 20 but she loved him with the innocence of a child. He was such fun to be with and, like her, he loved the animals, the insects and the flowers and birds. They were to meet again after the war when he was already married and she had lost her fiancé, Frank. Sven's marriage to Olaug, also a marine biologist, was one of convenience rather than love. They were friends and they married with the understanding between them that if either should meet someone else and fall in love they would be free to marry. And when Sven met Primrose again Olaug agreed to the divorce.

They married in the spring of 1950 and I was born two years later. We moved to Eiksmarka on the outskirts of Oslo and two years later Bertram arrived followed by my sister Yuli in 1956. My father, who was by now working for the Norwegian government as the fishery inspector for Norway, bought a beautiful old house that was in great need of repair on the outskirts of a small village near Molde. We children were strong and healthy, playing in the woods, rowing across to the islands to swim in the summer holidays or skiing and making snow huts in the winter. Then there was school, a long uphill walk and in the winter a great downhill homecoming on skis. An estate was built around our old house, Tondergard, and with our friends we went blueberry and mushroom picking and swapped paper serviettes that we collected.

In the summer I danced for the tourists that came into the Molde fjord on the cruise ships. I belonged to a small troupe of dancers at the Romsdal Museum. We were taught all the old Norwegian folk dances by Mali Furuness, a wonderful old lady whom we all adored, and a man called Jendem accompanied us on his fiddle. We all wore the traditional bunad, national dress, some from different districts, and my partner was Paul. I loved the dancing and we would also sing and then we would be invited on board ship for ice cream and fizzy drinks – such a treat! The Americans loved the fact that I could speak a few words of English so I felt quite important!

Then in 1960 Pappa took us all to America for six months while he was lecturing at the Universities in the North. When we came home he was ill, and so began his fight against cancer. It was a fight that couldn't be won in the early sixties; he endured five operations and months of excruciating pain, when we children would have to move quietly around the house as any jarring or vibration would be agony for him. As children, we didn't know he was dying and so it was a great shock when, one evening in December I was called in from playing in the snow with my friends to be told by my grandmother that Pappa had died. I was just nine years old. In the spring of 1962, Mum decided to move us all to England. With many of our friends gathered on the quay in Molde to see our ship off we left Norway in April bound for Dartmouth and a new life.

*

Many years later, after reading Pappa's story, I said half jokingly to my sister Yuli that one day perhaps we ought to do the walk. Through my work with the BBC, I interviewed the author Corinne Souza who had just published her book about her father, *Baghdad Spy*. After the interview I mentioned to Corinne that my father had been a sort of spy during the Second World War. She was interested and so I told her the story and sent her his account. She rang me two days later to say that I owed her a night's sleep and that I must get it published. She had been up all night reading it and when I also mentioned that we might do the route he had taken across the mountains to Sweden she urged me to do it. I'm so grateful to Corinne because it was her enthusiasm which fired me up to begin planning the trip. And then my Norwegian cousin, Anne-Margrethe said it was going to be the 60th anniversary in 2004. It had to be then.

*

Like all well-meaning plans nothing ever gets done until a date is fixed, and then you get a slightly panicky feeling that means 'you must do it'. There's no backing down, there's the general feeling of expectation that creeps in from all quarters and then you take a deep breath and go with it. Could we do it? Pappa had been ten years younger than we were and he had been supremely fit and knew the mountains well in all their unpredictability. Then when the doubts start to creep in you feel you can't let yourself down - it was just a joke, what a silly idea!

We first went for the end of June which was the 60th anniversary but then cousin Lauritz, Iacob's son, suggested that we might think about a later date as the weather was often bad in June and the mosquitoes might be too. So we picked the 26th July. Pappa was still walking at the end of July beginning of August so we were near enough. It was still nine months away and so we had plenty of time to prepare.

I went to the papers - the British press was decidedly unenthusiastic; he was a Norwegian, it was so long ago, they had already run a story like this and 2004 was the 60th anniversary of D-Day. The *Mail on Sunday* took it up, sent a reporter and photographer and then sat on it. However the Norwegian press and radio jumped on it. Through my cousin Sven, I met Jan Tystad, a Norwegian journalist from London, who came down with his wife and stayed the night. We became good friends and he has given me enormous support and encouragement ever since. He wrote a big article for the *Dagblad* and the *Romsdal Budstikke* which started the ball rolling. Very soon I was having phone calls and e-mails from people who had been involved in Pappa's escape or knew someone else who had but had since died. Those who had been children during the war came forwards with their memories. There was Kristian Finset who was aged ten at the time and whose parents Nikolai and Marit had reached out to help. There was Henry Berg and his family; Selma Moldsvor and her husband and brother who had been the first to give him shelter. Ragna Berg, Henry's wife, had run out to greet my father and said 'don't be afraid, we're here to help you'. And then there was Haldis who had been Pappa's housekeeper at Aukra and who knew about his secret work for the Allies and had played her own dangerous part in helping him before his arrest. Arve Oterhals wrote about the war museum on the island and how Pappa was heavily featured in it; Oddmund, an experienced mountain guide who promised to take us across the mountains from Isfjorden to Eikesdal, and Oerjar Heen whose father had also worked for the resistance. And there was Astrid Loeken, a well-known entomologist who had worked for the resistance and was a close colleague of Pappa's. There were so many, reaching out, offering friendship and eager to tell of their memories and their own stories.

My cousin Lauritz began to send maps of the route and I re-read Pappa's account with its detailed description of the direction he took. It was exciting as we plotted the route-plan and began to realise just how far we were going to have to walk. How easy or difficult it was going to be depended on the weather. Pappa had had to contend with heavy snow in parts, relentless rain and disorientating fogs when he lost his way in deep bogs and was frequently soaked to the skin. We had to be prepared for the worst. And so began the fun part of buying our equipment. Everything must be extra light and we had to keep it to a minimum. Two pairs of pants, one bra, one pair of trousers that could convert to shorts, two pairs of under socks and two pairs of thick ones, one pair of the best waterproof walking boots, the best waterproof, breathable anorak and one pair of waterproof, breathable trousers. Then there was the tent, sleeping bag, mattress, rucksack, other equipement plus a cover for when it was raining - Pappa had been offered a raincoat by one of his helpers but decided it would be too heeavy to carry. I was advised to take a GPS system to help to guide us but I found it too difficult to work with and in the end we relied on Yuli's new-found knowledge with a compass and map.

We would stay with Lauritz and his wife Ele for the first night, take the train to Andalsnes the next day and stay on the island of Gossen at Aukra with Haldis and her friends. Then back to Isfjorden where we would meet with Selma and her family before beginning our walk with Oddmund as guide for the first two days.

We started our training in earnest about a month before we left. I joined the gym and swam two or three times a week. I booked treatments with an acupuncturist and cranial therapist to make my back stronger. We walked and walked, every day, up and down the hills; the dogs thought Christmas had come early. When I started carrying the rucksack as well, I suddenly began to realize just what it was we were trying to do! The rucksack was heavy and made walking more difficult; I found myself slowing down considerably. And still I had to put more in. There was the food to buy, and heavy gas canisters and we would need fresh water at all times. But there was no backing down. We had said we would do it and Yuli and I never doubted that we could; we just had to be fitter.

* * *

We arrived in Norway on warm, sunny July day; the weather had changed for the better. We couldn't believe our luck. We found the bus from the airport at Torp to Shoelyst and were met by Lauritz. We also met Astrid Loeken, a friend and colleague of Pappa's who was an expert on bumble bees and had worked for the resistance. She was now 93 but with a sharp mind and very clear memories although she found it difficult to talk of the war and I had been told not to tire her too much. Over a meal I spoke to Astrid and asked her if she had been very afraid during the occupation especially as she had been so involved with counter intelligence for the Allies.

"No," she said, "I just felt ice cold all the time. It was as if I had no feelings about myself or my friends and family." Perhaps it was her way of coping. "We had to not let it get to us, when there was an unlucky thing and someone was shot in the night."

"Those of us who could speak German worked hard on it so that we could understand what the Germans said. We would give our information to our chief, Edward Bart, who wrote up the plans for the whole area and it would be sent to the XU headquarters," she continued, "and the films were sent over to Sweden. There was a person who would take all the information and photographs down to deliver at the railway station, and he had a code that he used. We had contact with people on the railways – it could be the conductor or the ticket master and they had a method of hiding the information. They went to the loo when the train began to move and there they would hide the packet in a secret place. They would then get word to Stockholm where someone would enter the train and retrieve the packet which was then sent to London."

Astrid's memories were so clear. She also told me she had been taken up to the woods at Skoyen where she had learnt to shoot with a pistol. Even her parents didn't know where she lived or what she was doing. She told them she worked for the newspapers. "I always phoned them before I visited, but they had to give me a very positive answer in case it was dangerous. After the war I went to America where I could be in a totally different environment away from my own country and where I could be myself"

*

The next day we were up bright and early to take the train for Andalsnes. At first the countryside was fairly flat and wooded with lovely flowers all along the way. Then slowly we began to climb, the train travelling at a steady pace all the way so there was plenty of time to watch the passing landscape. We marvelled at the glimpses of snow on the mountains, the waterfalls cascading down from the top and the beautiful painted houses, red, yellow and white and occasionally just plain wood. Norwegians love colour and have an innate sense of style which they use in their homes. Their textiles and paints are all in rich colours and they're not afraid of combining them to create a strong pallet and distinctive style.

Soon we were in the mountains and nearing our destination. There was the Romsdal's horn and the familiar Troll-tinnene which we had grown up with, all the mountains with their names that we knew so well. I always feel as if I'm coming home when I get to this part of Norway. It's the west coast with our home town of Molde just across the fjord, the place we loved and left as children but which still has such a strong hold on us. We wanted to experience again the mountains and the clean air and the freedom of walking through this wild landscape.

I had arranged to meet Arve Oterhals and Henry Berg at the station and although we had never met I knew them both straight away. Arve a tall man, well over six feet, with a firm handshake and a warm smile, and Henry in his eighties, his gentle face welcoming us. Also, there was Julnes whose father had worked with Pappa during the war. Henry showed us the quay where Pappa had first escaped off the boat which was moored alongside for the night in June 1944 and where he had walked calmly past the German sentries. It was difficult to imagine the danger my father had been in then as we stood there, 60 years later, surrounded by our new friends

Leaving Molde, we drove through more lovely countryside on a winding road with the mountains all around. Then we were on the ferry for Gossen, a short crossing. The island is surprisingly flat especially compared to Otteroy which lies beside it. This was perhaps why the Germans considered it important enough to build an airfield. They were convinced that the Allies were going to invade the west coast of Norway and Gossen became a strategically important position for them. They built the airfield along with prisoner-of-war camps and gun emplacements and by the end of the war had some 5,000 troops on the island.

We soon arrived at Marit's house where there were several people waiting to meet us. They were all so kind, beautiful smiling faces, people that we had never met who were all so welcoming, shaking hands, helping us in with our rucksacks and then offering us coffee and smorebrod in the beautiful Norwegian sitting room. It was such a joy to meet Haldis who had been Pappa's housekeeper while he was the director of the Fishing School at Aukra and who had helped him in his underground work. Well into her eighties but still full of fun and with an excellent mind, she carries her memories of Pappa and the time she spent at Aukra, recalling the moment he said to her with a twinkle in his eye, 'Haldis, if I ever grow up you must shoot me!' This was after he had again hoodwinked the Germans at great risk to himself.

Haldis told me she had found out about Pappa's work with the resistance after she heard him talk about it on the telephone. She was very excited to be helping him and was never frightened. "I don't think I had the right to be but you're not frightened when you're only 22 years old – it's very exciting." She went on, "I had contact with an engineer who worked for the Germans during the war and I spoke to him and told him he had to steal something from them. So he stole a map of the whole construction site – the airport. And he put the map on the wall. The Germans came to visit and searched and they never saw it and after they had gone I took it down and cycled over to Sven with the map and he sent it over to England. They bombed the airport two or three days later. They came very quickly – but I never asked why."

The following day we headed towards Isfjorden where we would meet the first of Pappa's helpers and where our walk would begin. This was the reason we had come back to Norway, to commemorate the 60th anniversary of Pappa's escape from the Nazi's and to meet the people who were still alive and who could tell us their own stories.

Sven Sømme

Sven's Story

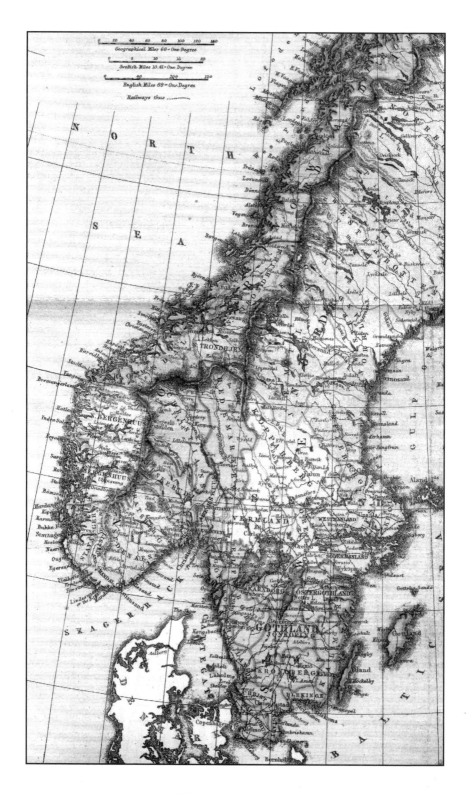

Chapter 1

OCCUPATION

SEPTEMBER 1940

Norway had been overrun by the Germans in 1940. I was in Oslo during the occupation, and saw it happen. In the weeks to follow we saw German officers and troops making themselves at home in our capital. We saw them marching through our streets, heard and hated the sound of their clacking boots. Their soldier songs sounded in our ears by day and by night. Their officers always shouted. We became fed up with their songs, their marching, their shouting and their smell. I believe it was their boots. There was a smell of harsh fat when they marched by.

Things had happened. Our newspapers tried to tell some truths. They were Nazified and their editors put in jail. They printed National songs, reprinted forgotten extracts of articles or speeches by well-known authors or politicians, which might hint to the present situation. They tried to resist, and were by and by silenced by rude force. We had read the German announcements:

"Shot he will be who ..."

Friends had been arrested, some for careless talk, some for secret anti-Nazi work. Secret newspapers had started coming out. Stories were told, and verified, of German brutality. Conditions grew slowly worse. Rationing .became more strict, sweets and luxury articles became more scarce. There was still no rationing of clothes. They had been so plentiful in Norway. There were plenty in stock. The Germans bought them with money they had printed themselves, sent underwear, gowns, silk stockings, suits, etc., in abundance to Germany, to wives, friends, parents, and so on; English clothing was mostly asked for, famed among the Germans for good quality. Suddenly there was nothing left. Everything sold out. Rationing was introduced when there was nothing left to ration.

The Nazi screw had started its ceaseless turning. For five long years it was turned slowly, slowly, and ever tighter.

In September I moved to Western Norway. I had been appointed Principal of a fisherman's school on an island at the Romsdal coast. It was a fairly big island, some five miles long and broad. You would not expect to find such an island in such a place.

In one of the most mountainous parts of Norway, where mountains rise to five thousand feet straight up, from the fiords, this island was almost as flat as a pancake. The soil was rich, people lived mostly from farming and fishing. They were prosperous self-supporting and happy. Not even the German invasion seemed to alter these conditions. People spoke angrily of the Germans having invaded our fatherland. They had seen the sea battles in the April days. They had seen the huge cloud of smoke rising above the mountains of the mainland when Molde, the town of the Roses, was bombed and burnt. The events had stirred them up for a while and then they returned to their old ways of living, their old problems of ploughing, sowing, harvesting and fishing. They shook their heads and talked about the bad news from the theatres of war. The Allies were driven back on all fronts. Britain was fighting alone. Sad news. Wonder whether Hitler is going to win the war after all. What a bad man, this Hitler. An old woman said somebody should go and *speak* to him.

It was thought more important to the people of Gossen that Peder was expected back from Vesteralen with a load of fat herring, and that Paul's eldest son had caught seven whales from his brand new vessel this season.

Near the Western point of Gossen was a German observation post, a corporal and six privates and a machine gun. They did not do anybody any harm. They just lived there, kept an outlook for Allied planes or ships at the coast, went to the merchant and the post office once or twice a week, and brought their washing to an old widow. That was all.

Such was the peaceful countryside I moved to. What

a difference to Oslo. What a relief from the marching and singing soldiers there and their shouting officers. Rumours of arrests and cruelties only reached us as a faint echo out here. Meat, milk, eggs and butter were abundant here. Everything was so rich and plentiful. The school was hardly a year old. It had been the pet of the Politicians from the district just before the outbreak of war, and had been started a bit prematurely with a preliminary Principal and before even the buildings were ready for use. The Norwegian war had delayed the final works, and this was what I had come to take over.

Everything was half fulfilled. The water supply was insufficient, the workshop was without tools and engines, a twenty-year-old motor and some worn batteries provided a scarce supply of electricity for lighting, and even the staff of teachers was incomplete. So there were lots of things to be done and all of them were urgent. They gave me sufficient employment for all the day and some of the night.

My home was brand new. It was a two storey red-painted wooden house, with white corners and window frames. I moved in with some old and some new furniture and tried to make a go of it. My wife was going to follow later in the year.

On my way to the post office I met a bright-haired, red-cheeked girl aged 20, firm looking but good-looking too.

"Are you the new Principal?"

"Yes, I am".

"My name is Haldis. If you need a house-maid I can take the job".

The bargain was settled, and I was never to regret it. I wrote to my wife that I had moved into my new house with a girl who spoke to me on the road. In her reply she sounded slightly worried. But she arrived two months later, on a dark rainy night. She and Haldis became great friends. How that girl could work! She cleaned the house, she unpacked and moved the heavy furniture into place, she cooked my food, did my laundry and kept everything in perfect order. From the bottom of her heart she hated the Huns. She wheezed when somebody mentioned Quisling or the Nazis, and she sang out to anybody who had not a clean political point of view. Her father had one of the biggest farms on the island. He was one of the cleverest fishermen too, a prosperous, intelligent and strong-minded man, with interests and knowledge far beyond the ordinary. His ancestors had lived in the same place for many centuries. He had modernised the farming and the fishing and rebuilt the old farmhouse. It looked more like an estate now than an ordinary farmhouse.

An old friend of mine was a teacher in Navigation at the school. We were the same age and came from the same town, educated as a Naval officer in the Naval College Arne Gröningsoeter had joined the merchant navy. When 16 or 17 years old he had rescued the crew of his ship after stranding. For years before the war, he had been captain on board a 15,000 ton American tanker, sailing between North and South America. In the autumn of 1939 he was called to Norway to serve as a Naval Officer in the Norwegian 2,000 minelayer Olav Tryggvassen which, on the night of the German invasion, sank a German minesweeper, made a total wreck out of the German destroyer *Albatross* and severely damaged the German light-cruiser *Emden.* When finally the battle was called off from the shore to avoid the town of Horton from being bombarded from the sea and air, Arne Gröningsoeter went ashore, got through the line of battle into Western Norway and settled as a teacher in the Fishery School. He wanted to be near the coast so as to get the chance of going across to Britain and continue fighting.

Well trained in handling people and tackling practical matters, Arne's presence was a great help to me in my somewhat difficult task. In his own quiet way, he advised me daily in important as well as minor problems. His wife and three-year-old son were also there. The three of them lived in Magnu's cottage.

We went fishing together every day. After lunch we went in Arne's rowing boat to look after our fishing tackle: some nets, crab pots, cod traps and sometimes we used a long line. It took us one and a half hours. It kept us strong and fit and it provided us with fresh cod, sea trout, coalfish, haddock and plaice, not to speak of big crabs and lobsters. I remember well one of these lobsters. It came up from twenty fathoms with the crab pot, which was a cement barrel with an entrance for the crabs at each end, but the lobster was not inside. It was a six pounder, and the entrances were too narrow. It was balancing on top of the pot, struggling to keep equilibrium there on the slippery wood, and when it came to the surface, it stretched both its huge claws towards Arne, who was pulling on the rope, as if to beg to be lifted on board. Its prayer was not in vain.

Happy days. Yes, they were, in spite of the German occupation, and all the sad things happening in our country, in spite of the bad news reaching us on the wireless from the world outside. We could not just sit down, hands in lap and cry. There was not very much we could do, except for some careful anti-Nazi propaganda among our pupils at school.

Every other Sunday, we went out shooting. Arne got hold of a tiny fishing vessel, 28ft. in length, with a peculiar four horse-power engine, home-made by a handy blacksmith in the neighbourhood. The owner of the boat went with us, and Arne was sometimes more interested in the manoeuvring of the boat and motor than in the shooting of the sea birds we were out for.

We always made a good bag on these Sundays returning home with loads of ducks, cormorants, herons and divers, providing food for our families for the fortnight to come. Sometimes we got one or two of the mighty great Northern divers, weighing up to 14 pounds. They too made good food.

About New Year we built a trap for catching hooded crows. One night after a heavy snowfall there were 27 crows in it and the next day 23. In a few months we caught more than crows in that trap. Arne and I soon became experts in skinning them and our wives in cooking them. They were absolutely delicious. We ate crows until we were near the point where we would wake up by night and cry 'kra-kra'. We taught the local people to eat them, we gave them scores of crows and our best 'customers' were the local Doctor and the Sheriff. Yes, we even sold our heaviest catches at sixpence a piece to a game dealer at Molde. He put them in a cold store and sold them later on for 1/6d.

The local Doctor was a tall, well built man with ginger hair. Health conditions were excellent in the district. He was a newcomer in the place and looked rather young. He always spoke straightforwardly to people. The fishermen and peasants were not used to that, so they had no confidence in the new doctor. He had little to do and he did not like unemployment. He did not like to sleep at night either so he used to come to me to chat the night away. It did not suit me, I had to work till midnight or longer and had to get up early in the morning. I used to join the pupils in their morning exercises at 7.45, so I just hated sitting up till three or four in the morning, talking with the red-haired Doctor. I was polite for two or three nights, then I was impolite, later on rude. One day I said to him: "I have eaten an apple a day now for a long time. I no longer believe in the use of it." "Why do you eat that apple?" "Because I have been told that an apple a day keeps the doctor away!" He sent me a fiendish look and stayed. When he knocked at my door next time I said "I won't let you in.."

"Please do, I'm bored sitting all by myself in that big house."

"I'm working, don't disturb me."

"Only five minutes."

"Go home to your knives and pincers."

"I'll work for you."

"I'm writing."

"I'll type for you."

"Damn you, get inside."

He typed for me till four in the morning. The following night he would mend my fishing nets till five. When nothing more was to be done he started embroidering. He was a bit of a carpenter and made a part of his own furniture. He carved nice things out of sperm-whale teeth. I never saw that man tired.

Molde and district

© Statens kartverk 2004

Chapter 2

THINGS BEGIN TO HAPPEN

One of our teachers did not do his work properly. He was an engineer, lecturing in engineering and also on workshop practice. He also planned technical improvements, and his job included the starting and running of the petrol engine for our own electric light. Very soon I discovered that I could not trust him. His schemes for water work were so inaccurate that I had to take over. When in winter the mornings became dark, he often overslept and did not start the power engine. I had to take that over. He did not run it by night either, so I ended up doing that too.

His salary was low. I told him that if he would do his work properly I would try to raise it. He said he would not do his work properly so long as his salary was insufficient. I tried to have him dismissed. His reply was to join the Nazi party.

There we were, he became the local Nazi leader; being the only local member, however, he had only himself to lead. He urged me to hang up Nazi placards in the school. That was according to orders from the 'ministry' and I had to do it. The pupils tore them down and I did not put up the new ones. So he complained to the Nazi Leader who sent me menacing letters, one after another. After a conference with the Chairman of the school's Council I put up some placards again. A gale swept them down and they were not replaced. Finally the case was treated by the Council of the school, strictly unpolitically. A petition to have him dismissed was sent to the 'ministry'. It was a delicate matter and the decision was delayed.

The pupils were wonderful. They did not turn up to his lectures, they teased him whenever they could, they drew the swastika on his cap and on the back of his jacket with chalk, and he wandered about the school innocent of the decorations. Finally he got tired of the whole thing and left us to offer his services to the Germans. A month later he was dismissed - by the Nazi ministry!

Arne confirmed his interest in the home-made engine of our small fishing vessel. One night we went over to a small island to shoot cormorants passing by on their way to their nocturnal quarters. There, behind the big stones, he told me about his plan. He would take his wife and his boy of three across to the Shetlands in that boat. Through weeks and months he had added gallons and gallons of oil to his store. He had rows of small boxes in Magnu's cellar, each containing a gallon of fuel or lubricating oil.

On 17th February, 1941, he disappeared with his family, one of the pupils and the boat. He took my rowing boat as well, because it was smaller and easier to row than his own.

It was well planned. He left on Saturday for a week-end cruise. He had obtained leave on Monday. On Saturday and Sunday he visited some of his friends in the islands, and on Sunday night he headed for another island but he did not arrive there. He made for the North Sea, although nobody knew it.

He did not return on Monday. When he did not return on Tuesday morning, I pretended to be anxious about what might have happened and I phoned the Doctor who was in the outer island that day asking him to enquire after Arne and his boat before he came back to Gossen.

I had a party in my home that night. Just after midnight the Doctor knocked at the door demanding an immediate conference with me. He was very unhappy. Arne had seen a friend at Flesa on Sunday afternoon and left him at 7.00pm to go to another friend at Harøy. He had told them he would pass west of Sandøy, which is a very dangerous water, filled with rocks and skerries. Nobody had seen any trace of the boat since. Pale, almost crying the Doctor told me this story urging me to do whatever possible to rescue the party in case the engine should have stopped and they were drifting there with no control of the vessel.

Nothing could be done that night so I waited until Wednesday morning when I telephoned the local Sheriff urging him to go out and search the waters with his ship. He was a good Norwegian. I gave him all the details known and he stayed out searching both Wednesday and Thursday. He came back with no better result than the Doctor and just as unhappy. We reported the sad event to the District Police Chief, he reported it to the Germans and the obituary of the whole family Gröningsoeter was read in the Friday newspapers.

I called the staff and pupils of the school to a solemn meeting and produced, deeply moved, a speech to the memory of the dead. I also included the nice boy, the young pupil, who had met with his death at a too early age. In the shade of this tragedy I said, we cannot go on with our work today and the school was dismissed to mourn the dead. Arne had been a beloved teacher. There was hardly a dry eye among the pupils, it almost broke my heart to make them sad, but it was necessary. If the Germans had any suspicion that Arne had gone across to Britain, not only would they confiscate all his property including a nice cottage near Molde, but they might also take reprisals from his relatives, from me and from the Fishery School.

When the funeral was over, I had a hearty laugh with my wife and life turned back to normal. I missed my friend but I trusted he had managed to get safely across and that he would soon be able to serve in the Norwegian Navy, something he had long been longing for.

More happened in May.

I had been to Trondheim on business and was on my way home on the coastal steamer. There was only one first class passenger beside me - a German officer. It was considered to be slightly risky to travel by coastal steamer. Some had been sunk by Allied aircraft or submarines. The German propaganda called that crimes, but actually they used the coastal steamers for carrying troops and they were armed with ant-aircraft machine guns. We did not blame the Allies for sinking these ships, even if we had to make use of them and wished they would not attack them.

The German officer and I did not speak together. We were sitting opposite each other all day in the smoking compartment, without exchanging a word. Even though more than a year had passed since the invasion I had never uttered a word to any German.

We both made preparations to go ashore as we approached the quay at Molde. We were just passing the ruins of the once so beautiful little tourist town, known by every Briton who has been to Norway. During the war it had been bombed and destroyed by German planes at the end of April 1940.

Suddenly the officer said to me: "Not very great damage done here."

"No?" I replied angrily "Only two-thirds of the town destroyed."

"The English did it," he said.

"No, the Germans did it," said I, and I felt my voice was becoming more angry.

"But there were military objectives," said the German.

"That is not true, not a single soldier," said I.

That was not quite true, but I understood he did not know. The Germans had a suspicion that King Häkon might be in Molde. That is why they destroyed it. And he was!

I did not see the Officer any more on that occasion but we would meet again.

As soon as I was back in school, we arranged a seminar, and I was enquiring of one of the pupils about some important zoological theme, when one of the teachers entered the room, telling me that two of the German officers wanted to see me. They were First Lieutenant Konrad and Second Lieutenant Schülze. They explained to me they wanted to see the school because they were ordered to confiscate a room for an office. An airfield was going to be constructed in the island and most probably it would prove necessary to confiscate the whole school shortly.

I showed them the school and told them that the only unoccupied room in the buildings was one situated between the two lecture rooms. It was not fit for an office. On the one hand people working there would be disturbed by the lecturing in the neighbouring rooms and if they were going to install a telephone there, their shouting would disturb the lecturing.

The officers decided on the spot they would not take the room, but they again said they would probably soon take the whole school.

I said I would protest against that, because this was the only Fishery School in the country, and I asked them which was their superior authority to which I might render a formal protest. They told me that was 'Herr Bube' at present presiding in the prayer house in the western part of the island. Then they clicked their heels, saluted and disappeared.

I decided to see Herr Bube immediately, got hold of a bicycle and found myself an hour later on the stairs of the prayers house. A guard led me to Herr Bube. When I entered the room he looked up and there was the officer from the coastal steamer, to whom I had shown my indignation at the German bombing of Molde! I think I managed to look as if I had never seen him before. He too showed no sign of ever having seen me before, though he must have recognised me. We were both coldly correct when I delivered my protest. He said he regretted very much, but he had his orders, and we would have to reckon with the confiscation of the school within a few weeks.

I went straight to Oslo to report to my superior Department, the Bureau of Fisheries. There was no Nazi there yet and I wanted the Department to protest to the German authorities against the confiscation of the school. They told me that would be of no use. The Germans were the masters and would do what they wanted, disregarding any protest. However, I wanted to fight for my school and finally obtained the Department's consent to negotiate with the German Authorities. I went to see Dr. May, leader of the Fisheries Department in the *Reichskommissariat*. He received me with utmost politeness. He was a handsome, tall man, hardly 30 years of age.

I had many good reasons for my protest. It was against the Hague Convention to confiscate a school of this kind, it was situated far away from the airfield, it was the only school of its kind in Europe, and the fishermen, who were so important to food production, might create difficulties.

Dr. May fully agreed with all my arguments, but he said very little could be done, because everything was decided by the military authorities. All power was in their hands. If they wanted the school they would take it, whatever reasons were against it.

I asked him to introduce me to the High Command.

Oh, he said, that would not be wise. If they happened to be in a bad mood, I might lose everything. If they were in a good mood, I might obtain the liberation of the school. The best thing to do was to render the whole thing to Dr. May. He would do his best and take the opportunity of negotiating with the High Command when they were in a good mood. That way he had the best hopes of success.

Back home I met with a surprise. Several German units had arrived in Gossen, and they had started bringing tools, engines, and workers to the island. That was not unexpected but they had taken the office that I had offered in the school and they had taken the pupil's sitting room as well. Oberleutnant Konrad had established his headquarters in a room in my home and taken another guest room for his 'secretary' a Norwegian girl Miss Nilsen. The pupil's sitting room had been filled with soldiers. The pupils were very excited and the soldiers had locked themselves in for fear the pupils might attack them.

I went into my office and wrote what I wanted to say to Konrad. I had no great experience in speaking German yet, and I wanted to be able to tell the Oberleutnant fluently in his own language what I thought about his action.

Then I went upstairs and knocked on his door. He was a bit confused when he saw me. I said: "I want to speak to you immediately in my office downstairs please." My spirits rose. I felt a bit superior now. Apparently his conscience was not clear.

We went downstairs, neither of us spoke until we were seated in my office. Then I delivered my speech, I reminded him of the first time we had spoken together, he had rejected my offer about the office in the school. I had left the school on important business confident that it was alright because the German Wehrmacht never deviate from their word, as the Germans had, assured us in broadcasts and in the newspapers. "Now," I went on, "what do I see? Not only have you taken the office you were permitted to take and which you rejected, but you have taken the pupil's sitting room as well, the only place they have got for themselves except for their bedrooms. I offered you an office and you have brought in a load of soldiers. Herr Oberleutnant, I am surprised and I expect you to withdraw the soldiers immediately and give the pupils back their sitting room."

First Lieutenant Konrad had been sitting while I was speaking, hands between his knees, his eyes fixed at some spot on the floor, like a schoolboy receiving a well deserved reprimand. I was surprised I had not expected a representative of the determined, victorious Wehrmacht to behave exactly that way. To tell the truth I had been frightened before I delivered my speech but I had tried not to exhibit it.

Now he looked up slowly and replied sotto voce: "The soldiers will be withdrawn within an hour."

I had won. I need not say I felt relief when they left.

An hour later two lorries took the soldiers away, together with their packs and wardrobes. The windows facing the courtyard were crowded with delighted pupils, laughing and waving to the soldiers.

The soldiers were furious but they could do nothing because the C-in-C, Lt. Konrad was there in person to see them go.

Chapter 3

THE VICTORIOUS WEHRMACHT

The final examinations of the school were soon to follow and when that was over the pupils would leave. I did not like to think what would happen when the buildings were deserted and my wife and I were left alone with the Germans.

The Germans kept their 'office' in the school. They made themselves at home there with a radio receiver. In the day the office was occupied by a sad looking German civilian who did not even try to look as if he was working. He was reading magazines and solving crosswords.

At night Konrad, Schütze and a naval officer, 'Kapitan Zur See' Neitschke, made themselves comfortable there with their girls. They had brought their own furniture, comfortable chairs and the like and they spent most of the night there, drinking, singing and shouting. Well past midnight, Miss Nilsen would leave them and go to her room, our guest room. An hour or two later, Konrad would enter the house, ascend the stairs and disappear into the same room.

The examinations were due to start on a Monday morning at 8.30am I had advised the pupils to go to bed early and get a good night's rest that Sunday night. At 11.30pm three pupils came and urged me to come down to the school and speak to the German officers. They were drinking and shouting, their loud-speaker was running at full force.

I went down. Nobody could sleep with such a noise. When I entered the office I found three officers there, each of them with a girl on his knee, some bottles and glasses on the table between them. The radio was howling they did not seem to appreciate my arrival.

I explained to them that the pupils were to have a difficult examination next morning, that they needed rest and sleep, and that their bedrooms were on the next floor, with poor insulation between the floors. I demanded that they put off the radio and stop shouting. Konrad replied, slightly irritated, that he understood the situation and the radio was put off. The officers promised to be quiet, and by the way, they were just about to leave.

An hour later one of the pupils came up to me again. There was no more disturbance by the radio but the Germans were noisier than ever, making it impossible to sleep.

Once more I entered the office and repeated my demand. Once more the Germans promised to be silent, and by the way, they were just leaving.

Half-an-hour later I made a round of the pupils' bedrooms. The noise was even worse than before. No one slept, some walked restlessly through the corridors, some were in bed trying in vain to sleep.

Once again I interrupted the Germans. This time my reception was positively hostile. Konrad shouted: "Come here and sit down." I did so. One by one the girls left. Schütze kept his girl company. Konrad, Nietsch and I were alone. Konrad found me a glass and asked me to drink. I hated the thought of drinking with them but the main thing was to obtain silence so that the pupils could sleep. Both the Germans were drunk. Konrad poured schnapps into my glass and spilt double the quantity on to the table.

"You Norwegians believe we are barbarians," he said.

I replied: "What reason have you to think so? Has anybody told you?"

He did not answer. Then he suddenly shouted. "We have treated you decently. I have seen your home. You have a nice sitting room and a lovely fireplace. If I wanted to I could confiscate it."

"Certainly, Herr Oberleutnant. You have got the power to take it and you know I cannot oppose you but you cannot expect us to be grateful if you don't do it."

Again he was silent for a while. Then the conversation turned to other matters. Every time one of the officers started shouting I said: "Please, quiet, Herr Oberleutnant"

"Please, quiet, Herr Kapitan. Remember the pupils need a rest."

After a while they started hissing at each other as soon as one of them raised his voice and the situation became easier. I had decided not to leave them until they had left the office. I sat there stubbornly for two hours. Meanwhile my wife had become anxious about my long absence, she was afraid something might have happened and finally came down to look for me. She stopped outside the office door and listened and she heard the following conversation:

Nietschke: "Herr Direktor, I have zhe gzheatest adm-ad-mizhachen for the Norwe-hic-ian sailors- -"

Director: "Please silent, Herr Kapitan. Remember the pupils please."

Nietschke: "I have zhe greatest adm" - and so on. She went back to her bed feeling much relieved.

The German military headquarters were at the school and the Bauleitung, the civilian office for the work in the airport, was at the other end of the island. Our dismissed Nazi teacher had been employed there. In our service he had administered the workshop. That workshop would, of course, be valuable to the Germans. We did not get his workshop key back when he left so the first thing I did was to change the lock to prevent him from getting inside. During the winter we had obtained tools and machinery.

One day, when I was away, a car drove up in front of the workshop. Out came Mr. Sørvig and four German officers. They went up to the door, Mr. Sørvig put his key in the key-hole and was disappointed. A message was sent to my wife. They wanted the key to the workshop. My wife replied she had no key and even if she had one she had no right to give it away. They sent for my deputy, Mr. Hanes, who hid somewhere in his house and his wife told them he was away on the moor getting peat for the next winter.

The officers apparently got angry and went away in their car leaving a disappointed Mr. Sørvig to himself. As soon as I returned, Mr. Sørvig and the officers were there again. A young Nazi boy was sent to my office.

"I have come to fetch the key to the workshop."

"Who are you and who wants the key?"

"My name is Anderson, Mr. Benel has sent me."

"Who is Mr. Benel?"

"He is the residing engineer at the airport."

"Tell Mr. Benel that if he wants the key he will have to come to me and explain what he wants it for."

A few minutes later young Anderson was there again.

"Mr. Benel shall have the key, that is an order."

"Did you tell Mr. Benel what I told you?"

"Yes."

"Tell him once more and make it perfectly clear to him."

Mr. Benel did not come. He left in his car with his officers and Mr. Sørvig was left alone once more. In the days and nights to come we evacuated the workshop of all tools and took them to a safe place. Only the heavy engines were left as we had no means of moving them but we took away the spare parts.

Gossen by and by changed from a peaceful peasant land into a German camp. Several hundred Norwegian workers were brought to the island, gathered from all parts of the country, partly forced to work there, partly tempted by the high wages. Barracks were built close to the place chosen for the airfield. Lorries, cars and engines of various types arrived daily. Soldiers and officers arrived to protect the island. Areas were closed to civilians, pill boxes and gun emplacements were constructed.

There was only one main road leading from the two small piers on the eastern side of the island to the north western part where the airport was being constructed. No good piers existed in the western side of the island. Everything needed for the work had to be landed at Aukra in the east and brought by lorry on the main road leading to Løvik in the west. This road had not been built for heavy traffic, there had been only one small lorry and two cars in the whole island before the Germans arrived, and the roads had mostly been built for the peasant horse traffic.

Now we had evidence of the famous German administration! After a fortnight's heavy traffic and some rain there was not much left of the road. It consisted of mud and deep holes. Lorries stuck in the mud, or their springs broke, or they tried to evade the mud by driving alongside the road and sank in the marshes.

One lorry after another had to be abandoned. Our red-haired Doctor, who employed all means of transport for his visits to his patients used to say: "It takes three hours to get to Rød by car, two hours by bicycle and one to walk."

The Germans made no attempt to mend or rebuild the road in spite of their calculation that it would take them two or three years to complete the airfield. They covered the worst places with planks or truckloads of stones. Soon more than 200 vehicles used this five mile stretch of road, and after three years use the road was permanently in a state of disrepair and steadily deteriorating. If the road had been rebuilt properly at the beginning millions of kroner might have been saved, not to speak of time. Later on a harbour was constructed near the airfield but it took a very long time before it could be used.

There were three authorities in the island, the Norwegian Sheriff, who had the civil administration, the German civil engineers who constructed the airfield (*die Bauleitung*), and the German military command, who administered the soldiers and the fortifications. These three departments were always quarrelling.

I was once called as an interpreter between the later German C-in-C Major Vogt, the Norwegian Sheriff and the residing Engineer for the construction works, Herr Fuehrer (yes, that was his real name).

The cause of the disagreement was a Norwegian driver in the service of the Germans who had become tired of getting in and out of his lorry to open and shut the numerous gates blocking the road. The gates were there to keep the sheep and cattle away from the corn and potato fields. He drove full speed through all the gates smashing them one by one into matchwood. Drivers were scarce so he had to be handled with care. He was neither punished nor made responsible for the damage he had caused. Sheep had eaten all the cabbages belonging to a farmer and he claimed compensation of £5. The Sheriff represented him at this memorable meeting.

Major Vogt and Herr Fuehrer both agreed that compensation should be given to the farmer and that his claim was reasonable considering the damage that had been done. The Sheriff also put forward a claim that £15 should be paid for the gates that were destroyed. There was full agreement on this matter also. Finally the Sheriff suggested that the system of gates should be abandoned and replaced by cattle traps, that would allow vehicles to pass without trouble, but prevent the cattle and sheep from getting through. They would cost about £25 each and 20 such traps would be needed. That would make £500.

The Germans found this to be an excellent idea. In fact speed was essential in the construction of the airfield and cattle traps would save time.

Herr Fuehrer finally told the Sheriff that the money would be paid by the military authorities, as this was a military matter, but Major Vogt rose from his chair and claimed that this was a matter of construction, so the money should be paid by the Bauleitung. The Sheriff asked me to tell the gentlemen that it was a matter of indifference to him who provided the money but unfortunately that did not solve the problem.

Both Germans were fairly large men and during

the long quarrel which followed they turned more and more pink and their voices became louder and louder. Finally they sent for a German lawyer, who was probably employed there to settle questions like this between the two authorities. His arrival however seemed only to stimulate the quarrel. So the Sheriff asked me to tell the party that he had to leave now and he would be grateful to learn where he could get the money when the question had been finally settled.

Very high wages were paid to the labourers in the beginning and extremely high wages to the lorry drivers, most of whom were Norwegians. They were paid by the hour. Money was plentiful, there no control over how it was used. Some drivers took advantage of this in writing up more hours than they had actually been working, and in some cases the drivers were paid £10 per day, for 24 hours work, every day for a whole week.

Housing and sanitary conditions in the camp were beyond description. The floor of the canteen kitchen was made of ribs with open spaces between them. Rubbish of all kinds was simply dropped between the ribs till the space under the floor was filled up with a stinking mass. There was no lavatory. The men just went 'round the corner'. Water for washing and drinking was collected from small ponds between the barracks. When it rained, as it often does in this part of the country, water 'around the corner' was washed into the ponds that provided the drinking water. Food was bad and insufficient. No wonder, therefore, that shortly after the erection of the camp there was an epidemic of dysentery and a severe decline in the general state of health, and even some cases of death.

The insufficient food and the high wages caused a black market to flourish. The peasants sold their produce to the labourers, and the prices rose rapidly. Standard prices for butter and pork were £1.50 per pound, two shillings were paid for an egg, £10 for a bottle of spirits, cigarettes were a shilling each, an ounce of tobacco was £1 and so on.

In brief it was a Wild West camp.

But so were the German Headquarters at the school in the beginning. When the pupils left towards the end of June, the Germans confiscated most of the main school building. One of the lecture rooms was turned into a dormitory for the soldiers, the other one into an officers' canteen. The bedrooms were partly used for their original purpose, partly used as offices.

In general, the soldiers ration of spirits never came further than to the officers, and they had great drinking parties twice or three times a week. It was impossible for my wife or myself to sleep on such nights, even though our house was 60 or 70 yards away from the school. The officers and their girls, the latter collected from various parts of the country, were shouting, singing, quarrelling, smashing windows and furniture. Later at night they would vomit from the windows at first floor down to the cemented platform beneath! That sound did not make the neighbourhood more agreeable.

Until 26th August, 1941 we were allowed to keep our radio receivers. When the pupils were still there, they used to come to my room at 7.30pm to listen to the Norwegian news broadcast from London. They filled the sitting room and the verandah outside. The

Germans passed by and were fully aware of what was going on, but they never interfered. Our house being built of wood, the broadcast could be easily heard from the sitting room on the ground floor to Konrad's office on the first floor. Schütze was also often sitting there. We took advantage of this in providing them with the German news from London at 9.30pm and they could not avoid hearing every word of the propaganda through the floor.

One night the three bosses, Konrad, Schütze and Nietschke passed the windows of our bedroom at two or three o'clock, when my wife and I suddenly were woken up by Nietschke's drunken voice shouting in English: "Zhis is zhe Bzhitish Bzhoadcasting Corporazhen."

It was meant for us and he repeated it still more loudly to make sure we got it. We did, Nietschke had got his revenge.

Herr Nietschke, Kapitan zur See, was a peculiar person. He must have been about 55 years of age, short and broad, looked like an ordinary ship-mate. He would seem jovial and broadminded to those who met him for the first time, but he was the most unreliable person I ever met. When Konrad and Schütze were away, as sometimes happened, he acted as C-in-C and he always tried some dirty tricks.

One day in July, Schütze came to my office, complaining that it was very cold in the school. He wanted our porter to light the central heating and to borrow fuel from us. We used peat for burning, I said we had none left, and none was to be had as far as I knew. He might ask the Sheriff whether he knew of any way of getting some (I knew the Sheriff was a good Norwegian who would not provide the Germans with anything, if it could be avoided).

Schütze left.

Half an hour later, our porter, a nice man and strongly anti-German, came to me in excitement, asking: "Have you told the Germans to order me to light the central heating for them, and use our peat?"

"Who has given you that order?"

"Nietschke did."

I told him about my very recent conversation with Schütze, and said he should never obey any orders from the Germans, but refer to me if they gave him any trouble.

Konrad returned in the evening, I went to him immediately and reported what had happened, again referring to what the propaganda had told us about the justice and honesty of the Wehrmacht. He promised to treat the case properly and to prevent repetitions. I also claimed that no German should have any right to give orders to my people, and that all negotiations should be carried out between the C-in-C and myself, and not between our subordinates.

Better still, he stuck to it. I told my subordinates about the agreement and we never had any more difficulties of that nature again.

Nietschke apparently was thinking about revenge because he did not get his own way over the central heating. One afternoon when Konrad and Schütze were away again, a former pupil who stayed with us in the summer as a handyman told me that Ludvig, the porter, had been arrested.

A few days earlier, Konrad had told me they had to turn one of the cellar rooms into a prison, in case something should happen, and he asked me if I had a key to that special room. I sent for the blacksmith who was an old friend of mine.

We had tried to use that room as a store for potatoes, but it was too damp as there was something wrong with the ventilation, and we had to give it up.

When the blacksmith arrived, I asked him to make three keys. One was to be given to the Germans, I kept one myself and gave the third to Ludvik.

As soon as I heard about Ludvik's arrest, I went to have a look into the cellar. Quite right, there was a sentinel patrolling the corridor leading to the cell.

I went upstairs to Nietschke.

"Why has Ludvik been arrested?"

"Has anybody been arrested? I did not know about that."

"But you are the officer responsible at present?"

"Yes."

"Then you should know about it. And if you don't, I suppose there is no reason for his arrest."

"No, there must have been some misunderstanding."

"Then I suppose he is free?"

"Certainly."

"Please come with me to the prison."

And poor Herr Nietschke went with me to the cellar. The sentinel saluted and Nietschke ordered him to open the door. I said: "Ludvik you are free and may go home." "And by the way, Herr Kapitan, will you please inform your subordinates that our people are employed by the Norwegian State, and that they may not be given orders by your people. Everything shall be settled by agreement between the Oberkomandant, Oberleutnant Konrad and myself. Is that clear?"

"*Jawohl*, Herr Direktor."

Chapter 4

THE GERMANS TAKE OVER

My wife did her best to limit the officer's rights in our home. When, late at night Oberleutnant Konrad came to visit Miss Nilsen, he was rarely sober. The stairs leading to the first floor were not silent either. The combination of Konrad's riding boots and the squeaking stairs was not agreeable when we tried to sleep. Konrad soon learned which steps were most noisy, and avoided them by taking two steps at a time, but in spite of that precaution my wife always heard him. One morning she said: "Herr Oberleutnant, would you mind taking your boots off before you go upstairs? They always keep me awake."

And Konrad did, though it certainly hurt his officer's honour.

Then she said, "Would you mind using the lavatory at school instead of ours? This is a private lavatory you see."

Konrad again obeyed.

My wife had some minor skirmishes with Miss Nilsen as well, but always behaved with the utmost correctness. The result was that in the long run Konrad and his mistress did not thrive in our house, and shortly after the pupils had left both of them moved to the school, where there were fewer restrictions.

It was a relief to get rid of them, and as soon as they had moved, my secretary, who had previously occupied a room in the school buildings got Miss Nilsen's room. She had just moved in when a German soldier entered my house without knocking at the front door, went upstairs and straight into my secretary's room without even knocking at her door. I had heard him coming ran after him and caught him just as he entered the room. Miss Legernaes had just started dressing and was not at all prepared for a visit.

"What are you doing here?"

He looked utterly confused, clicked his heels and saluted.

"Excuse me Herr Direktor, Oberleutnant Konrad ordered me to fetch some small things he had left in the office here."

"This is not his office. I have brought these things down to the school. And next time you come here will you please remember this is a private house. Knock on the door and wait until you are allowed to enter. Understood?"

"Yes, Sir."

He again clicked his heels and disappeared.

Five minutes later he was there again. He knocked at the front door. I waited to see what would happen.

He knocked once more, and I let him in. Salutation again.

"Excuse me Herr Direktor. I am sorry to trouble you again. But we could not find the things in the school, so Oberleutnant Konrad asked me to ask you where they have been put."

"They are in room number five." More salutations and that was that.

This was my first experience with a German soldier, and I had evidently hit the right way of treating him. Actually the soldiers did not show any respect as long as I called myself 'Schoolmaster', but as soon as I started employing the title 'Direktor' their respect increased accordingly. It was of no use whatsoever to try to speak politely or with friendliness to a German soldier. That was regarded as a sign of weakness or fear, and only produced rudeness. But given orders - the stricter the better - they always obeyed immediately, politely and almost humbly. This discovery amused me, and whenever an occasion occurred I employed the method successfully. Although I was a civilian, even the officers obeyed me provided I gave my orders firmly.

In the beginning, the soldiers took liberties such as stealing rowing boats to go across to some of the neighbouring islands to bathe or to collect birds eggs. One afternoon four of them had taken my boat. I got another boat and rowed after them, telling them that they should go back immediately and leave the boat where they had found it. They just laughed at me and used vulgar language.

I reported to Konrad but could not give the names or the numbers of the soldiers. He lined up all his men in the courtyard and I pointed out the guilty ones. They were reprimanded sharply and given some hours punishment exercise. It never happened again. I told Konrad that the soldiers took boats belonging to fishermen and farmers too, and I told the people to report to me whenever a boat was taken by Germans without permission. Soon there was an end to boats being taken.

The school had its own waterworks. There was a well in the valley below the school and a petrol motor pumped the water up to a concrete tank on a hill behind the school. The water ran by gravity to all the tanks in the buildings.

We had been allowed two gallons of petrol a day to run the pump and we used a little more than half-a-gallon a day.

When the Germans took over the main building, I told Konrad that they used too much water, and that we could not afford sufficient petrol to keep the pump going. Konrad asked: "How much petrol do you use a day?"

"About two-and-a-half gallons."

"Suppose we provided the petrol, could you please run the pump for us?"

That was just what I wanted, and we got three gallons a day. Actually we managed to run the pump with our own rations, so we stored what we saved from the Germans. When the first barrel was full we rolled it to the sea and stored it in a boat-house and started filling number two.

About 20th August, 1941 Konrad told me he was going away. Major Vogt had come to take over the command and he introduced me to the Major.

Only a few days earlier I had had a cable from the Fishery Board asking how much of the building we needed for the next course. Obviously this was a result of my negotiations with Dr. May at the Reichskommissariat, and I had thought that now we would perhaps get most of the school back. I replied that we could do with the main building, the workshop and some of the auxiliary buildings. There was an old impractical timber building with a number of bedrooms too. I hated that building and thought that we might leave it to the Germans if they insisted keeping part of the school.

My first conference with Major Vogt was a disappointment. The General, he explained, had visited the airfield, and he regretted very much to inform me that they would soon have to take over the whole property of the school, including my home. In fact, he was sorry to say that we would have to move within a week. But we could take every thing away with us, except some beds, chairs and tables belonging to the school.

If necessary he would let some of his men help us in the packing.

Before the telegram from the Fishery Board arrived, I had been expecting the confiscation of the whole school any time, and had taken steps to secure other accommodation in another place.

Major Vogt was a short, somewhat fat man, rather good looking and definitely cultivated. His attitude towards the Norwegians seemed to be very friendly.

That night I went to a sandy beach just below the school to dig for sandworms as bait for my long line. It was a warm bright summer night. Several German soldiers and civilians working in the offices were at the beach enjoying the beautiful night. They were always loaded with curiosity, and I could hardly do anything without being asked by some German what I was going to do.

Some soldiers passed me.

"What are you digging for?"

I turned my back to them to show that I did not want any conversation, and heard one of them saying: "Hush, it's the Direktor." They disappeared without any further inquiries, and I went on digging.

Three civilians came by.

"What are you doing?" I turned my back on them without replying. "Digging for rainworms?"

"No."

"What is it then?"

"Something better."

"What is it then?"

I had been raging internally for some time, but now I

could not keep my fury back any longer and shouted: "I am digging a mass tomb for all of you."

I just saw their heels as they disappeared uphill, heading for the school. I knew they would report to the Major, and I felt this was the beginning of the end for me. I had behaved like a fool and felt like one.

Early next morning I heard someone knocking at my front door and entering the hall. There was the sound of firm steps and a rattling of spurs. It was the Major in person in his most brilliant uniform, sabre at side, epaulettes and golden laces.

"I must speak to you immediately."

He did not look amiable.

"This way please."

I led him into my office. We never allowed any German to enter our sitting room.

"I very much regret that my first visit to your home is on a disagreeable matter but I have received an official report about you, and it is my duty to deal with it in an official way."

I thought the best thing to do was to try to make the whole thing humorous, and I laughed as heartily as, under the circumstances I was able to.

"You are here about the scene at the beach last night Herr Major?"

"Yes that is right and to me it is quite a serious matter."

I admitted I had said something which I would never have uttered if I had not been aggravated, but it was meant as a joke, and I was quite surprised to see it was not received as one. Certainly the German sense of humour must differ from the Norwegian's, but after all, there was a certain amount of vexation in my remark. I then explained to the Major how week, after week, after the arrival of the Germans, we had never been allowed to do anything privately, without being asked by curious Germans what we were doing. For a long time I had been patient, trying to show the Germans that I did not want conversation. So far, I had never uttered an unfriendly word but the Germans would never understand that we wanted to be left alone to ourselves. Last night there had been just a little too much curiosity and I had lost my temper and said words that I admitted I should not have said.

The Major replied that he had tried to explain to his people that it was only natural that I lost my temper last night, because I had been told that the school and my home were going to be confiscated. He also wanted to tell me that his people had complained many times to him that the Norwegians were cold and unfriendly.

Judging from our history, our shipping and our mentality however, he fully understood that our sympathies were directed towards the British, and that we could not be expected to regard the occupants with friendly feelings. Vogt himself was a representative of the occupants and he did not like it. Norwegians must, however, realise that they are occupied. As for himself, Major Vogt considered it as his duty to try to maintain the best possible relations between the occupants and the occupied. Norwegians therefore must do their best to behave correctly and he would do his best to make the Germans do the same. What happened at the beach last night was definitely incorrect and such a thing must not happen again.

I promised to guard my tongue thereafter but repeated that we did not like the German curiosity, and asked him to tell his people that Norwegians wanted to conduct their private lives without always being asked by the Germans what they were doing.

The Major promised to do so and he kept his word. We were never again worried by untimely questions. Conditions improved after Vogt's arrival. The drinking orgies ceased, or at least became rare. There had been ordered rooms for several German officers, in Norwegian homes in the neighbourhood, and privately they went on drinking and were a nuisance to their hosts.

Minor irregularities still occurred, however, and I had to report to Major Vogt on several occasions so as to maintain my good reputation among the soldiers and employees.

There was for instance, a kitchen garden belonging to the school the Germans sometimes harvested the wine berries and blackberries there. I reported to the Major and he put an end to it.

My crow trap was taken by the Germans for their hens. They had five chickens there. They were fed on sea water and biscuits and were sick and miserable creatures. I claimed the trap back and won it. The chickens were moved to another place where they ultimately died from ill treatment.

They kept rabbits too. When finally I dismantled my crow trap, some of the netting wire was taken by a Corporal Siegler. He converted it into rabbit cages. I reported it to Major Vogt as a case of theft, committed by a member of the super-honest Wehrmacht. Corporal Siegler happened to be away on leave just then, but I did get my wire-netting back, and Siegler was said to have been punished on his return from leave.

I spent the whole summer of 1941 guarding our property and our minor rights. Every day brought its problems, its quarrels and its small pleasures in vexing some subordinate German. Unfortunately we had lost the great battle, the battle for the school. By and by the German grip tightened. More rooms were taken, our movement and rights were cut down. On 26th August we had to give in our radio sets to the Sheriff. My shot gun, my 22 rifle and a Colt Woodman pistol went the same way. The Germans decreed that every family all over the country should give a blanket each to the occupying forces. Of course we delivered the oldest we were able to find. Some people cut holes in them before they were delivered. The blankets were paid for but at almost nominal prices. All tents and parts of tents had to be handed in. Only a very few were given, we hid most of the tents as they might be useful some day. All rucksacks were ordered in, again very few were delivered, some simply kept theirs others burned them. Rubber boots had to be delivered. This order did not come out any more satisfactory for the Germans than the tents, blankets and rucksacks.

The last days of August were very busy ones. I had only our porter and one of the former pupils to assist me in packing all our things. We worked very hard. I went to the Major, telling him that we could not move at all unless we had lorries to take our things to the quay and a ship to carry them away. He offered me a vessel called Nordsol. I knew the ship and said it was too small. Then we obtained a bigger one, an old barge of about 100ft. We had six soldiers to assist us in packing, and two big lorries. The soldiers were lazy and we had very little done by them, but the lorries were useful and took all our belongings to the quay. They also took a barrel of petrol which we had saved by the water-pump agreement. The first barrel was still in the boat-house, and we could not get at it with the lorry so we had to leave it for the time being. A young officer turned up one day. He had come especially from Trondheim to offer us barracks for the school, and he told me that these barracks were very well fitted to serve as accommodation for our school. I said we had decided to move to the neighbouring island, Otterøya, and did not want his barracks in Trondheim. He raged and said it was an order. There were sufficient bedrooms for all the pupils, there was central heating, a modern kitchen, dining room, sitting rooms, lecture rooms, and it was all new and well built. I still refused to take them, having the feeling that there was something rotten about it. I explained that this was a district school, and that the fishermen all along the coast would object to having the school moved to another county, that a school like this one could not be placed in a town, and I had many arguments of similar kind.

The young officer turned red and told me he was going back to report and that I would hear from him again. I never did.

I made some enquiries about the Trondheim barracks. My suspicion was justified. The school would have been situated near a German camp and they wanted to use us as protection against Allied attacks! If we had been hit in a bomb raid they could claim that 'only civilian targets were hit' and 'civilian lives were lost', etc.

We moved on 30th August. The previous day Major Vogt asked me, "Where are you going now?"

I told him we had got part of a council school at Midsund on the island of Otterøy, some 14 miles southwest of Gossen, and I showed him on the map where Midsund was.

"Why," he said, "that is a dangerous place. The Canadians will get in there and take you over to Canada."

I said I had always wanted to see Canada.

"But haven't you got fortifications outside there to prevent a landing like that?"

"None at all. So they will take us to Canada as well, as prisoners."

"But what are you going to sing then? You cannot sing *Den wir fahren nach England* when you are actually going to Canada."

"No," I replied sadly, "we will sing *It's a long, long way to Tipperary.*"

"Well goodbye then, see you again in Canada!"

We had become fond of our school, of our home and our garden. For eleven months we had worked hard to get everything in order. We did not leave with pleasure. Sure enough it would be a relief to get away from this German delirium but I hated handing over to the Germans all we had produced with the work of our own hands.

My house had been built in an old meadow. We had turned part of it into a garden of our own, planted and sown, seen the flowers shooting up, the brown soil being covered with grass, vegetables and flowers. In the autumn I had prepared a big strawberry garden. This summer we had cut away all the blossoms in order to obtain strong plants which would yield a good crop of strawberries next summer. Papavers and sweet peas were in full bloom. I also had a field with tobacco plants that were not fully grown yet, but they had to be harvested.

West of the house we planted apples and other fruit trees in a large field. They had rooted and were in full leaf just now.

The day before we left I called Bruun, who had been a sort of handyman to us and ordered him to take a scythe and cut down all the flowers and vegetables. The blooming garden was turned into a desert. The Germans saw it happen but they neither asked nor interfered but we saved the fruit trees and the strawberries. After all, the next year the Germans may have been thrown out, and the garden might be ours again.

When I visited them the following summer they had appointed a special gardener to take care of the garden and I saw him, with my own eyes, carrying loads of my beautiful strawberries into my house, which had been turned into an officers' mess.

Chapter 5

WE START AFRESH

We arrived at Midsund at 9.00pm on the 30th August and had finished the unloading of the ship at 1.30am in the morning.

The next day I was confined to bed with an acute appendicitis. Under normal conditions the new course should have started on the 1st September, but owing to the removal we had to postpone it until the 14th. I was operated on on the 3rd and was back to work on the 11th and opened the school on the fixed date. The new conditions were a bit primitive. The pupils were living two by two in small rooms in the houses of the village, as kind of paying guests, and the local people were marvellous. One of the two merchants, Kristian Oppstad, and his wife, moved out of their own bedroom in order to make room for pupils. He, with his wife Milla and daughter Ingrid, took on the task of giving 25 of the pupils a substantial lunch every day in their own home. Like most people they had a fair supply of food stored away to be able to meet future demands. Now they used all of it for our pupils, most of whom had never lived as well at home before the war.

The teacher of the Council school, Sverre Voile and

his wife Emma, took over the lodging of three of the teachers, including my wife and myself, and provided dinner for about ten of the pupils. Five of the pupils had their homes or relatives in Midsund, and stayed and had their meals with them.

Otterøy is about ten miles long and four miles broad. It is entirely different from the neighbouring island of Gossen being mountainous and wild. It is almost like a square piece of wedding cake, the cream representing the mountain peaks in winter time covered with snow, the edges representing precipitous hills, rising in general to 1,500 ft. Along the shore is a narrow strip of low land and there are small farms all along the edge of the island. The interior of the island is filled with lovely old pine forests and barren mountains but there is not a single inhabited place, except for a few *seters* where the farmers take their cattle in summer to let them benefit from the rich pasture of the mountainside.

Midsund is at the western point of the island. The sound between Otterøy and the island of Miøy further west is narrow and forms a well sheltered harbour. Farms and houses surround the harbour, and there are two merchants, each of whom has his own warehouse and a stone pier.

Most of the inhabitants are fishermen and farmers. They have a piece of land, a cow or two, some sheep and many of them have a modern fishing vessel of 40-60ft. The whole population of Midsund may be perhaps 200. A greater part of them have the surname Midsund, and a fairly high percentage of the masculine inhabitants has Iver as a first name, while a somewhat lower percentage is given the name

Olav, which gives rise to confusion. But the good inhabitants of Midsund have a practical system to avoid confusion. The surname is omitted for daily use and the persons are named after where or how they live. There is Iver-in-Lynga, Iver-on-the-Hill, Iver-in-the-Moor, Iver-in-Gjerdet, Olav-in-the-Meadow, Olav-on-the-Telefone and so on. Their wives are sometimes named the same way, sometimes after their husbands. Jørgen Anna, for instance, is the wife of Jørgen. So it is all very simple.

All the farms are painted, wooden houses, none of them are more than two minutes' walk from the sea, but the teacher's house is cast of concrete, yellow painted and situated just below the 1,500 ft. precipice. It is a big two-storey house with a flat roof and an enormous open veranda around three sides of the second floor. My wife and I occupied that second floor, which consisted of a single big room with fourteen windows and a brilliant view of the harbour just below, the fjord to the south and the ocean to the north west. We could watch the fishing vessels coming and going, and we could watch the big convoys passing by on their dangerous journey along the Norwegian coast. Situated higher than any other house in the village we could look down upon our neighbours and see what they were doing. When we turned round, we had the precipice above us, and it seemed to hang over the house, ready to bury us at any time, but it never did. Sometimes some stones fell down with much noise, but they did not come near us. Some small burns fell vertically from the edge of the precipice into the rock-falls below. After rain the whole mountainside was almost covered with a veil of water. In strong western and north-western gales the waterfalls were thrown back over the edge and disappeared. I often wonder where all that water was stored because we could not see it coming down.

The council school was situated almost at the same level. It was a low modern wooden building. We had a fairly big lecture room in the basement and a smaller one on the ground floor. Also in the basement we had a tiny teacher's sitting room. It was inconvenient because the only connection between the basement to ground floor ran through it and between the lectures there was a never ceasing traffic of people passing through. On the ground floor we had a room 6ft. by 10 ft. to shelter our zoological, botanical, geographical, chemical, physical and medical collections and equipment.

That was all. The rest of the building, which was the other half of the ground floor, was occupied by the council school. I was given an office 10ft. by 10ft. in a neighbouring house.

Then we started to work.

Chapter 6

AN ILLEGAL NEWSPAPER

My wife was working in Oslo that autumn. Oslo was the centre of events. There were the Gestapo Headquarters, the Quisling Government, the Reichskommisariat and the German Military Headquarters, and near Oslo were the notorious concentration camps Grini and some smaller camps plus some political prisons. Oslo was also the centre of the resistance movements. The well known struggle of the Church, the University and the teachers were centred there. A great number of secret national newspapers were also edited there. My wife kept me informed of the various events, and from time to time I received a number of illegal newspapers.

In our quiet countryside very little happened. Everything just seemed to pass on normally. To the farmers it was far more important that Iver's cow had got twins, than the news that six or seven hundred teachers had been arrested and deported to the Finnmarken district.

Weather and fishing were more important than the declaration of the resignation of the Bishops, Deans and Pastors of the whole country. Nobody was ever arrested in the countryside. Maybe the daily controlled

German newspapers did their silent work too, anyway, people did not realise what was actually happening in our own country. They shook their heads when they talked about the atrocities of the concentration camps, but in their hearts they did not understand it, because they had no first hand information, and because they did not know personally any of the victims.

Several radio receivers were still in use. Everybody listened to the Norwegian news bulletins from London. Everybody was anti-German and was disgusted by the steadily bad news from the various theatres of war, and everybody was delighted to hear about the important part the Norwegian Merchant Navy was playing in the war. Churchill's speeches also encouraged us and made us feel confident in a final Allied victory. There was not a single Nazi within the whole parish. Apart from shortage of coffee and tobacco life was fairly normal and food was plentiful.

The secret newspaper that reached me told day by day what was actually happening within the country. I received only one copy of each and even if I let it circulate among the population here I could not reach the large number of people in the other coastal communities, so I decided to print my own paper.

There was a good duplicator belonging to the school, but only one typewriter which was in daily use in the office and could not be used as it was easily recognizable.

The first thing was to get another typewriter, paper and stencils. The duplicator had been bought by the school for duplicating circulars and text books.

Now I obtained the consent of our Nazi ministry to buy another typewriter, 1,500 lbs. of paper and several hundred stencils, all this for duplicating text books. I also bought rubber gloves and heaps of different envelopes, vast amounts of stamps and went to work. I typed the stencils at night, printed them employing rubber gloves, folded the sheets, wrote the addresses in various ways, and was surprised to find how many variations a typewriter permitted. For instance Oslo may be written in the following ways: Oslo, OSLO, Oslo, OSLO, -Oslo-, etc.

Combining this with different colours and sizes of envelopes, with different space between the lines, and in placing the lines differently, it is easy to obtain so many combinations that a hundred letters all look different.

The point was to avoid control of a large number of similar looking letters, which might be suspected to contain secret newspapers.

Postage was 20 øre, and I varied the postage as much as possible. First there were three different issues of 20øre stamps. Next I might use 10 øre or 5 øre stamps in various combinations.

Finally, I could use either of our two official languages, *landsmal* and *riksmal*. Indeed when I spread out the finished letters you would hardly have thought they originated from the same sender.

The first issue had no name. It contained mostly articles taken from other secret newspapers, mixed up with some reflections of my own. It consisted of three sheets, six pages, densely printed and it opened with an article by Sigrid Unset: '*Ja, vi elske* ...', 'Yes we love ...', the three first words of our National Anthem.

In order to post the letters I went to one of the nearest towns, Ålesund, the letters were wrapped in a parcel inside which was a heavy piece of iron. It sometimes happened that the local steamers were examined by the police on arrival in Ålesund, therefore I stayed behind until most of the passengers had gone ashore. If any of them had been examined I would have dropped my parcel alongside the ship and it would have sunk to the bottom.

Nothing happened, however, and I went ashore. I had a good friend in Ålesund. I went to his office with my parcel, unwrapped it there, and put all the letters in various pockets. So I went from one letter box to another, around the whole town, and posted approximately ten letters in each box. If I had posted the whole lot in one box it might have been noticed by some Gestapo or informer, and I might have been searched. Every now and then I walked through side streets to see if anybody followed after me, and I felt relief when the last letter had been posted.

Thus the letters were spread all about the district. I knew several reliable people and friends supplied me with new addresses. I also sent a copy to myself in order to control whether the letters reached their destinations which they always seemed to.

I soon realised that my paper ought to have a name. Of course I should have called it 'Yes we love' but that name did not occur to me. My imagination stood still. All the good names seemed to have been taken by my greater colleagues. I had nobody to consult. A very good underground paper in Molde was called *V-Posten*. Damn it, I called mine *Q-Posten*. It did not occur to my mind then that Q was for Quisling, nevertheless I stuck to that name later on. My paper was not a Quisling paper anyway.

In the beginning I tried to issue my paper every day. At 7.30pm I listened to the Norwegian News Bulletin from the BBC referring as much as possible. I went home and pretending to be occupied with urgent office work, I typed, printed, folded and enveloped during the night. At least twice a week I went to Molde or Ålesund to post the letters. They must not be stamped 'Midsund' because our duplicator was the only one in that place and could easily be traced. But sometimes I posted the letters on board one of the local steamers, or asked the skipper, whom I trusted, to post them in Molde. He knew approximately what they contained.

Besides the news I always had small articles of my own, or articles from colleagues. I also had the pleasure of seeing that one of my political reflections "The Plight of Sweden', was printed by my colleague *V-Posten*.

I soon realised that I could not afford an issue every day so I made it twice or three times a week, or more irregularly. It was rather expensive, each issue cost me 10 or 20 kroner in stamps and sometimes more.

One night I was printing as usual in my office when I noticed that one of the sheets fell out of the pile while I was duplicating but I forgot it.

On my arrival in the office the next morning the secretary greeted me with excitement. "I thank you so much Mr. Sømme, I was so thrilled to get it. Oh it was so kind of you. Please do let me help you."

"What is this all about, what do you mean?"

"The newspaper, *Q-Posten*! Oh, I was delighted. I thought it was for me."

My secret had been revealed.

My secretary wanted to assist me. I could trust her, and there was plenty of work. I had to get the news, write the articles and type the stencil myself. But she might duplicate them, fold them, and, yes, post them. Why not? I had enough to do in school, my frequent journeys to the neighbouring towns took lots of valuable time. She could do it.

She really saved me a lot of work. She got her instructions and went to Ålesund to post the letters. She was a bit pale on return, but happy she had performed the task, a few days later she went on her second expedition with a bunch of letters.

When she came back that night she was very unhappy. "I am so sorry Mr. Sømme, I can't do it. It was horrible, I saw people following me everywhere. I nearly fainted when I saw a policeman. I am so unhappy, I can't do it, I can't do it."

That was the end of that, I had to take over the posting again. My secretary went on with duplicating and folding the sheets. Poor girl, I did not know then that she was sick. Shortly afterwards she had to leave the job and she stayed at home and in hospitals for two years.

My wife was at home for the Easter holiday in the spring of 1942. I had an uncompleted job to finish. There was still that barrel of petrol at Gossen which we had saved from the Germans and hidden in the boat-house. I wanted to fetch it. My wife joined me.

We went in the motor-boat the usual way to Gossen. The weather was bad, it was snowing heavily on our way to our former home, it was so bad we could not see very much. We were both sitting in the cabin in the front of the boat trying to identify skerries and islands as we went along. There was a steering wheel inside the cabin so we were comfortable there.

In Gossen we went up to the merchant, who was an old friend of ours, he seemed very surprised.

"Are you here? How did you come?"

"In our own motor-boat."

"But have you reported your arrival?"

"No, why?"

"There is a curfew on. Some labourers left their work and escaped. The island is closed. Nobody may arrive here or leave the island except by special permit. Vessels approaching or leaving without a special permit will be fired on and sunk."

"Well nobody fired at us."

"Which way did you come?"

"Kjaerringsundet"

"Gosh! It was mined two days ago, there has been a warning in all the newspapers."

"They have not arrived in Midsund yet!"

"What are you going to do now?"

"We have got an invitation to see Tøge."

Not a soldier was to be seen near the pier. So we went on board again and left for the north-western corner of the island where Tøge was living. That part of the island was not guarded by the Germans.

We spent two pleasant nights and a day with Tøge and his family, then went back again to the merchant. I got two men to take the petrol barrel out of the boathouse and roll it into the sea. It was too heavy to be carried directly on board. In the meantime I went up to the C-in-C to ask for a sailing permit. Major Vogt had left some time ago and another Major named Oloffs had taken over. He was said to be a rough fellow but I did not meet him. The Major was away and there was a Captain in his place.

The school looked worn, everything was dirty. The road leading up to the school was covered with planks, it was muddy underneath, just like the road to Rød.

The Captain was impolite. After some negotiations I got the permit. It read:

'*Der Sømme Sven ist gestattet, trotz mines Verbotes, der insel Gossen zu verlassen*' or translated:

'Sømme Sven is permitted in spite of my prohibition to leave the island Gossen'. Place, date, signature, and then the remark: "This permit is to be handed over to the guard, who shall again deliver it back to the military headquarters."

I asked for a permit for my wife. She could not get one unless she went up there in person. I did not know where she was just then. We were going to meet at two o'clock at the quay and the office closed at 1.30. It was closing time when I got my permit.

We met at 2.00pm and took the motorboat to the boathouse. There were the men and the barrel was just floating. The German headquarters were just above us but nobody there seemed to take any notice of us. We took a rope around the barrel and towed it to the quay. We could use the crane there to haul it on board. There was a sentry too so I called out to him: "Hey, Fritz, how are you? Fine weather, isn't it? Will you lend us a hand in getting this barrel on board?"

'Fritz' looked surprised. He was not used to being spoken to in friendly terms by Norwegians, still less in his own language. But his face brightened in a broad smile and he handed me the rope and pulled the crane. Gosh, he was a strong fellow! Up came the barrel and he lowered it again nicely into the boat. With a grin he stretched out his hand for the exit permit, then folded it to put in his pocket. I wanted to keep it as a memory of the event and stretched out my hand to get it back. Indeed I got it and he did not ask for my wife's which did not exist.

When we left he was waving to us with a broad smile. He had met friendly Norwegians.

Chapter 7

A FRIEND PAYS A VISIT

SPRING 1942

I do not know whether *Q-Posten* really did any useful work but I am quite convinced that national propaganda was much needed in my district. Sometimes I had the pleasure of hearing people saying: "I have read it in *Q-Posten.*"

The pupils read it. One of them was a fine chap whom I fully trusted. He had been fighting in northern Norway in 1940, had been wounded and was partly invalid. He liked to get the news every night and was quite unhappy when it sometimes happened that he could not get it. He had a good memory and a fine brain so he sometimes noted down the news headlines when I could not get it myself.

I handed my own copy of *Q-Posten* over to him together with the envelope and he secretly passed it on to other pupils. Nobody knew where it came from. There was never a single Nazi among the pupils.

One day a friend of mine wrote to me from Oslo and suggested giving a lecture at the school. The lecture was a success and he stayed for a couple of days. He used his right name for the lecture but he travelled under a fake name.

After a careful examination of my attitude to politics he told me of his plan to use me. He wanted me to join the intelligence service and to organise this service within a major part of my own and the adjacent counties along the coast.

I hesitated, certainly, I wanted to join the service but I was very busy with the school and the paper and there would not be much time to spare for the intelligence service. He said I would have to drop my paper as this work was far more important and I would not be allowed to go on with the paper if I joined the intelligence as that combination was too risky

True enough, I had a certain opportunity for travelling and we had just bought a motor boat for the school but I only knew a very few people to whom I could entrust this top secret work. The organising would claim a fair amount of work. I did not know whether I could spare the time for it. The school was a new one and my lectures were on new matters. Text books had to be written and there was plenty of work in providing the necessary food. Also I knew nothing about military subjects.

He said he did not know anyone else in the district who might do the job. I would soon pick up the necessary military knowledge. After all, if after some time I felt that I could not do the whole job I might take over part of it.

Finally I agreed to try. We spent two days discussing

details. I learned about my future work, how to distinguish German units and ranks, how to form a report, and what had to be embraced by the reports, how to prepare invisible ink, how to use it and so on. I learned the main principals of the organisation, how to avoid suspicion, all the necessary precautions in field work, in brief, how to become a spy. Then I went to work.

It was not as easy as I had thought. First of all I had to get in touch with reliable people, I knew a few, and I had a few addresses. In Ålesund, I was put in contact with the wrong person. I had the wrong Christian name. He did not dare take the risk. He was married and he had to consider his wife and children. Later on I learned that I had been shadowed when I left him. That was because he had thought I might be an informer or a German agent. I did not have much better success in the other towns of my district.

In one town, however, I was put in touch with a first class fellow. What a brain, what spirit, what courage. Yes, and what a wife! He was the editor of a secret newspaper which was delivered almost every day to most of the reliable citizens of the town, and to large districts outside the town. His wife assisted him. They had a little girl and were living two or three miles outside the town in a small cottage. They picked up the London news every night by a receiver which he had stolen from the Germans. The whole set was hidden in a biscuit tin. When listening to the news he made short notes on a piece of paper. Afterwards he was able to recall them word for word surprisingly correctly. They produced the paper at night. In the morning he went to his office, his wife did the housework then went to town, taking the baby with her in a pram or in a basket on the bicycle. The paper was underneath the baby. In town she distributed it to sub-distributors, and the 'subscribers' had the paper about lunchtime every day.

He bought me very good things, and I passed them on to headquarters but too many knew he edited that well known newspaper and he was arrested, his wife too. She was released after a short time as she was expecting another baby.

I only learned later about his arrest because I went away that same day to serve as an expert in a trial within my speciality. My second course in the school had finished, and I had some holiday for the first time since my arrival. Of course I should have gone into hiding when he was arrested. Most prisoners who were supposed to know about someone else were taken to long and trying examinations. They might last for 60 hours or more, during which the prisoner was very hard pressed and almost invariably tortured. Some were able to withstand even the severest torture others were brought to talk more or less unconsciously. Therefore, it was a golden rule that when one member of an organisation was arrested the others should go into hiding for some time. Three months were considered the minimum.

I do not know how my contact was treated but I know his life was in danger for rather a long time, and that he was supposed to be a spy. Other prisoners taken on the same occasion were released or sent to Germany, he was kept together with two men who were also under suspicion of gathering intelligence. That was a very bad sign but he did not utter a word about anyone.

One day I received a letter from his wife:

"Thank you so much for your letter. I would like to discuss things closer with you some day, as soon as it is convenient.
Kind regards, Marie'

It meant: 'Come to town for an immediate conference. Danger.'

We met 'casually' in the street. She said: "We don't know each other. You are just asking me for the way to the church. Understood? You are in danger. I have been visited twice by a man named Mattiesen. He has been in prison together with my husband and has been asking me twice about you. I believe he is an informer. He boasts too loudly about his merits as a patriot. He arrived in a German vessel after being released from imprisonment. He does not know anything about you yet. I have told him I do not even know your name, be careful. Goodbye."

I received another letter later, and went to town. This time we were able to speak together for some minutes. She told me that she had been visited by Mattiesen again. He had told her that he had information from reliable sources, but very secretly that her husband had been court-martialled and sentenced to death. He was still in the same prison camp. If she could get a driver to take him from the camp to the Swedish border, Mattiesen would manage the rest of it, that is, the very act of escape.

He came to see her again later. This time Mattiesen said that if she could provide £25 he would arrange the escape and get her husband safely across to Sweden.

I asked her what she had replied.

"I do not *buy* my husband from the Germans!"

"But now," she asked me seriously, "Do you believe that it is true what Mattiesen has told me? Do you believe that my husband has been sentenced to death?"

"I don't know what to believe, but I do not trust Mattiesen. This may be another dirty trick to soften you up for some reason. He may hope that you will give him useful information from sheer despair."

She told me that every three weeks she went to Trondheim, asking the Germans to be allowed to see her husband. She never received permission. Then she used to go to the prison camp. Once she had seen him. He had become thin and his hair was more white but his spirit was unbroken.

All the time she had spoken quietly, business-like. Her voice was calm, there were no tears in her eyes, not the slightest sign of external excitement. I knew she loved her husband. But how could she leave her children for four days every three weeks only for the hope of getting a glimpse of her husband if she did not love him?

I met her again a month later. She looked worn and tired, but, she spoke just as calmly as when we met a month ago.

The Germans had sent her a parcel containing her husband's clothes without a word of explanation. She contacted the Germans but they would not tell her anything.

"Do you believe this means they have killed him?"

"I don't know what to believe, it may just be an act of terror. You are regarded with suspicion and they may want to scare you. If he had been tried and shot I see no reason why they should not have published it."

"They have sent the other two prisoners to Germany. Their wives have been informed about it, but there is no news at all of my husband."

"Let us hope that no news is good news."

Still some time later on she got a letter from him. He was in Germany. Prisoners sent to Germany were considered to be comparatively safe. They were probably not tortured any more. Their case had been decided but only seldom was there a sentence.

Chapter 8

SECRET WORK

My attempt to organise the whole district given to me was unsuccessful. I organised the nearest districts that was all. I was too occupied with my work at the school to be able to travel as much as was necessary. So I asked to be released from the whole district and be left with only my own particular part of the coast. That worked much better. I was able to learn more details about the fortifications and the German movements in the immediate vicinity. I was glad to learn later on that the whole district by and by was organised as well.

I specialized in photography. They sent me a 'Leica' with all the necessary equipment, including a telescopic lens. I practiced taking pictures through a buttonhole in my coat. After a while I became so used to that I could get fairly good shots that way, even with the telescopic lens. Of course these pictures had to be taken near the Germans, and sometimes there was a certain amount of excitement about it. I felt comparatively safe as long as I was at sea. If anyone thought they had seen me photographing and stopped me I could drop the camera and the equipment overboard. My boat was so small that the Germans did not take much notice of it and it passed the German positions so often that they soon learnt to recognise it. There was a zone of in general 400 metres round each position where no vessel was allowed to enter. The small local steamers often made short cuts through these zones. The Germans knew these vessels because they saw them every day, and they regarded them as harmless, but I knew the skippers of these vessels which was useful. Sometimes I asked them to go as near a certain position as possible and from a hidden position on board I took valuable shots from various angles.

I always kept in touch with the Germans in Gossen. They had taken various items belonging to the school and I kept on asking them to give us back some of them. There was for instance a blackboard. We had long negotiations about that, and it gave me sufficient excuse to go to Gossen twice. Then there was the petrol motor for the dynamo. The Germans had installed power engines of their own. Later on they got a connection to a power station far away and became independent of petrol engines. That gave me an occasion to claim the motor for the water pump as well. Then there were some tables. Wood for such things was unobtainable because the Germans used all our wood for military purposes among which was covering roads in the rural districts.

Soon we had all these things back and it was not easy to find new excuses to visit Gossen on business. Then the rumour came that Major Orloff had removed his HQ to a somewhat remote and insignificant farmhouse. He was said to suffer from a barbed-wire complex; wherever he was living he always surrounded his place with vast amounts of barbed-wire.

I wanted to know whether this rumour was true. So I went to the German *Bauerverwaltung*, which was in the main school building. There I explained to them that the school owned a piece of moor in Gossen where we used to take peat for our heating. Now we had no peat in the school, nothing at all to burn, but we had plenty of peat in Gossen. Our problem was to get it over to Midsund. We could provide a ship to take it across the sea but we had no means of getting it from the moor to the sea because the Germans had all the vehicles. Would they lend us a lorry for that purpose?

This was apparently a serious problem. The *Bauerverwaltung* could not decide it. I would have to ask the C-in-C about it.

"But I am not permitted to go to that part of the island"

"We'll give you an introduction."

So they did, and I went happily along. Of course I did not get the lorry but I found out that the rumour about Major Orloff was true. He was living in a very small farmhouse which was hardly visible through the enormous piles of barb wire. And after all we had plenty of peat at Midsund.

I had Haldis back. She had been to a Commercial College, and this time she came as my secretary.

One day she said to me: "I have been engaged to a civil engineer. He is working at the airfield in Gossen and now they are going to send him to the Barnak airfield in Finnmark. He does not want to go but he

Sven Sømme, hunting in the
mountains before the war

*The Somme family (left to right): Helene, Knud, Sven, Iacob,
Prof. Somme, Helene, Sigval Bergesen, Ingrid.*

Pre-war pistol practice

The Fishery School on Gossen where
Sven was Principal in 1940

The ruins of Molde after being bombed by German planes in 1940

Sven pictured in Oslo during the war

Ragna and Henri Berg

The torpedo station at Klauset which Sven was photographing when he was arrested

The barn in which Sven hid at Erstaddalen

*Sven and his helpers take a break in the mountains
during his trek to Sweden in 1944*

*Sven tree-leaping to avoid leaving
footprints in the snow*

Sven and Primrose on their wedding day 1950

Sven with Bertie, Yuli and Ellie 1958

is forced to. He wants to go to England and fight. Can you help him in getting across to Sweden?"

"I suppose I can, but on one condition: If he can get me a map of the German projects at Gossen, I will provide him with certain introductions. This is top secret."

I had the map. Later on I found out how her fiance had obtained it. First he had asked the Germans for a copy. The request made them mad and they made a great fuss about it. So he stole it. He was going to Oslo first. The day he was leaving Gossen the Germans turned up in his room and searched him. They examined his luggage, his papers, his drawers, everything, but they did not find it. He had hung it on the wall so it was fully visible to everybody who entered the room. When the Germans left him he took it down, folded it and put it in his luggage.

He had an introduction to a friend of mine in Oslo, who had been taken to an examination by the Gestapo a few weeks before, and had been on his way to Sweden later on because he and his organisation thought the Gestapo knew about his underground work. At the last moment, however, he had been called back. His conversation with the Gestapo had been carefully studied by his organisation and they had drawn the conclusion that the Gestapo did not know anything.

In reply to my letter of introduction, which did not mention any names, my headquarters in Oslo sent me an urgent letter, reproaching me that I had not sent the man directly to them and asking whether he was reliable. I had collected information about him so I could safely reply that he must be regarded as fully reliable. I learnt later on that he had not been sent to Sweden after all. He had joined the Secret Service of my organizataion and had gone to Finnmark as ordered by the Germans, but not to do exactly the work they wanted of him.

Who took part in my work?

It is certainly not right to mention names and actually I only know my own little circle in my district. But they were farmers, tradesmen, teachers, civil engineers, employees in the local administration, in brief all kinds of people. Most of us did not know each other. None of us knew who was above us or whether there was a single leader on top of the organisation or whether it consisted of separate, independent units. We did not want to know. That would mean danger but each of us had a deputy who knew the work intimately and who could take over in case we disappeared. And all of us had an individual number which was used instead of our name. Each of us had a false name too and our correspondence was always addressed to that name. Our correspondence would look innocent to any observer. A typed letter about ordinary things, business, or a message from one friend to another. Between the lines were the real messages, written in invisible ink.

Most of us certainly knew too little about military matters but we received directives and information from our HQ. Thus we eventually evolved a routine.

Photographs, printed matter, etc., always went by courier. Now and then we were visited by an inspector who introduced himself with certain passwords.

We used 36mm cameras. In order to explain what could be seen in the photographs I used to project the negatives on a piece of white paper, draw the contours of the landscape or whatever it would be in china ink, noting the particulars on the sketch, then photograph the sketch again. Thus the explanation was also reduced to 24 by 36mm and could be easily transported.

I used to work at night in my room on top of the teacher's house, some times accompanied by my deputy. I used certain scientific work as an excuse for my photographic outfit and nightly work and I do not think Mr. or Mrs. Voile ever had an inkling of what was really going on there.

In October 1942 my brother Iacob, who lived in Oslo, was arrested by the Gestapo. He had devoted himself fully to secret work. I knew his work was important but I knew no particulars. He had been warned that his arrest was imminent and had left his own flat sometime before he was taken. He stayed with friends and probably he remained in Oslo to be able to complete his work. Finally he was seized in his own flat just as he was there for a short visit. He was taken to the notorious concentration camp Grini near Oslo.

Shortly after his arrest my sister Ingrid had to go into hiding, an informer had reported to the Gestapo that she had been involved in Iacob's work. She hid for six weeks with friends and then escaped into Sweden.

People who were informed about conditions at Grini told me that Iacob's case was very serious. He had been a dangerous man to the Germans. We also received reliable reports that he was repeatedly tortured. Again and again he was brought from Grini to be examined at Victoria Terasse, the Gestapo Headquarters in Oslo. Later on in Stockholm I met one of his fellow prisoners, who had been in the same cell as Iacob for ten months. He told me that sometimes when Iacob had been to an examination he was brought back to the cell more or less unconscious. Sometimes he did not even know his own name or where he was but he recovered. There was a German guard at Grini, who made it his speciality to ill-treat my brother. His name was Unterscharführer Kuntze. He used to order my brother to the door of the cell then flap his gloves several times just in front of Iacob's face. If my brother stirred he would kick him or beat him. If not he would flap Iacob's nose with his gloves until it started bleeding.

On 17th November, 1943, Iacob was tried and sentenced to death, 'for having placed his knowledge and abilities at the service of the enemy'. In December we received, by official channels the message that he was not to be killed. He would be kept as an important witness in case more should be learned about the work he had done. Then on 3rd March, 1944, he was suddenly shot. My old mother had seen him at Grini only two days before. He had learnt then that he was not to be executed. He had been in brilliant humour.

When Iacob's closest friend informed me about the death sentence at the end of November 1943 I had for some time felt less safe myself. My mail had been stopped. No letter arrived for three weeks, except my secret correspondence, which came to my fake address. It was a horrible time. Any day I expected to hear that Iacob had been murdered. Any night I expected the Gestapo to arrive. It seemed so difficult to get away. I had the school and I was responsible for food for forty people. Much of that had to be bought on the black-market and I would not entrust it to others. I could see no reason for an immediate arrest unless some informers had reported about me. I felt that every one of my steps were shadowed by some invisible observer. A bad cold had set my physical condition back and I felt my nerves were getting worn.

For the Easter holidays I went to eastern Norway to enjoy skiing and to try to regain physical strength. My wife Olaug came up from Oslo and we met at Atnasjøen. I had crossed the mountains between the Gudbrandsdalen and Atnasjøen on skis. I had crossed them before but now I wanted to learn more details about this part of the country in case I had to escape that way across to Sweden. For the same reason I wanted these holidays at Nesset. If I had to go to Sweden, I wanted to pass here, get rest and get further supplies for my journey. Hjalmar was an old acquaintance. He was a young farmer and I knew I could trust him.

We had a wonderful holiday in Nesset, every day we went skiing in the forests and mountains. We studied game birds, we found and photographed footprints of the 'glutton' a greedy, predatory mammal, which preys on reindeer. We found the dancing place of the heavy capercaillie and one day we saw a fox. We also caught trout and char with bait through holes in the ice, and we had a glorious time. I felt my strength coming back and felt fit to resume my secret work. Olaug was going to stay a few days longer after I left.

She accompanied me to the watershed when I went back across the mountains. It was a dull day with heavy sleet. The snow was wet and clung to the skis. I had to cover 30 miles across to Mysuseter. Just below the watershed we had a picnic, we had sandwiches and cold mutton cutlets and a thermos flask with delicious cream. During our meal the flask fell over and broke. It looked like a bad omen. Were we to meet again and where?

I stood at the watershed for a long time watching my wife sliding down the valley back to Nesset, she turned and waved back just before she disappeared. We met a hundred days later in Stockholm.

Chapter 9

THIN ICE

That winter I did not dare to go out shooting at sea. Many people knew that I still had a shot-gun and I wanted them to forget it, I also spread the rumour that I had sent it back to the owner. Seabird shooting could not be done secretly. The boat would be observed, the shots heard. I started hunting Germans instead.

The Quisling Game Laws granted the same shooting rights to Germans as for Norwegians. That meant they had to have a permit to carry a gun, pay for a shooting licence and they must have the consent of the landowner to shoot on the land. They had to obey the law and not kill protected game and not shoot in the protected seasons. The Germans did not worry much about restrictions. Only a very few Norwegians knew that German shooting was restricted and fewer still took the trouble of reporting illegal shooting. So the Germans took advantage of this ignorance and went shooting wherever and whenever they wished.

One restriction was the shooting of sea birds from a vessel driven by an engine closer than two kilometres to the nearest shore.

Eiders were protected all the year round all over

the country. They were very tame and before the Germans came to Gossen there used to be thousands of eiders in the Rinderøy Sound, in the harbour and along the piers of the little Rinderøy village. The Germans machine-gunned them, killing hundreds and wounding hundreds more. The officers roared with laughter at the poor wounded birds trying to escape their motor-boats. Eiders were easy to shoot because they were so tame. They were a type of pet to the fishermen's homes and used to nest between the boat-houses. They soon became scarce.

I would report to the local Sheriff and to the nearest German position whenever I saw illegal shooting. The villagers at Midsund used to report to me when Germans were shooting, and their shooting was always illegal. If it was not in the protected season they were shooting eiders, and if they were not shooting eiders they were shooting too close to the shore from a motor-boat.

Mr. Voile, my landlord, the local teacher, was the local Parish Gamekeeper. When I saw or heard about illegal shooting I would call for him. We jumped into the motor-boat belonging to the school, and went out hunting Germans as we called it. We had a brand new powerful diesel engine, and could make nearly eight knots. The German boats were usually former Norwegian fishing vessels and could only make six or seven knots. The crew were mostly Norwegians.

We used to run up and stop the German vessel. Mr. Voile could not speak German, so the conversation was left to me. I would say, "This is the Parish Gamekeeper, I am his interpreter. Your shooting is illegal."

"Of course not," they used to reply.

I asked for a gun permit and receipt for shooting licence, but they never had any. Then I told them what was illegal about their shooting. They never had any idea about the Game Laws.

I demanded names, ranks, station and so on. They would never tell us but we always knew pretty well where they came from and told them so. Finally I told them that their shooting would be reported to the police and to their superiors. Then we went home and prepared a report for the police. Voile signed it. I signed as a witness. Then I phoned the German authorities in question, informing them what had happened and demanded that they inform their subordinates about the Norwegian Game Laws.

We never heard what happened to the poachers afterwards but they did not poach any more in our neighbourhood.

One day Peder rang me up: "The skipper of the tug *Karl* has just shot an eider female at our pier. That eider was the only one left here. It used to swim about here every day and we used to feed it."

I telephoned Voile: "German poacher again at the pier."

"I am coming."

The skipper was wandering about calmly on the deck of his ship when we arrived.

"Are you the skipper of this tug?"

"Yes."

"We would like to speak to you."

He led us downstairs to his cabin.

"This is the Parish Gamekeeper, I am his interpreter and Director of the Fishery School here. It has just been reported that you have shot an eider. Is that so?"

He looked utterly confused.

"No, not an eider, it was a düker."

"Your name please."

He gave it. Age, home address, employer's name and so on.

"Have you got a permit for carrying a gun?"

"Yes, at Åndalsnes."

"And don't you know that you must always carry it about with you when you are hunting?"

"No."

"Have you paid your shooting licence?"

"Yes but the receipt is at Åndalsnes."

"Can you produce the bird?"

"Yes, of course."

He disappeared up the stairs and returned with an aluminium pan containing what was left of the bird, cut to pieces.

"Where are the skin, head and feet of the bird?"

"Thrown overboard."

I pretended to examine the pieces carefully.

"Well, Herr Kapitan, this is an eider."

"No, it is a düker."

"I am sorry to disappoint you but I am a zoologist and I know the birds here. There is no other bird with a carina sterni like this one, such carini are only to be found in the Genus Somateria."

"But, Herr Direktor, it is a düker. This bird was brown and the eider is black and white."

"I am surprised Herr Kapitan. You are shooting in a foreign country without a permit, without a license. You shoot in the protected season, even the düker is protected at this time of year, and you do not even know the game you are out for. Right enough, the male eider is black and white but the female is brown and this is a female eider. They are our tame house birds, protected throughout the year, it is murder to kill them. Your first duty when you go shooting is to know and to obey the law and to know the game you are out for."

We found a brown feather on the floor.

"Did this belong to the bird?"

"Yes."

"It is a feather of a female eider."

When we told the skipper that he would soon hear from the police he looked very unhappy.

We produced a report to the police accusing the unlucky skipper of breaking five points of the law. Voile signed it and I wrote a PS stating that I had examined the bird, and, being a zoologist I found the shape of the carina sterni proved it to be an eider.

Professor Knut Dahl was staying with me at the time and he added another PS stating that he had examined the feather and there was no doubt it came from a female eider. He signed the PS Knut Dahl, Professor of Game at the Agricultural High School of Norway.

The formal document was handed over to the police. We never saw the skipper of the *Karl* again.

I had no permit to carry a gun and I would not ask the Nazi authorities for one. Before the German invasion any Norwegian might carry a shotgun without a special permit. I still regarded it as my legal right to do so. I went shooting too, but I respected the closed season. Otters were not protected and were quite numerous in our district. They used to go ashore near the German torpedo station at Klauset two miles from Midsund. In the early spring I watched their tracks in the snow and went out by night to shoot them when they went down to the sea after dusk. I got three otters there.

The beginning of May was the black-cock and capercaillie season; at early dawn they perform their peculiar plays and dances in the mountains and forests. There were several black-cock and a few caper about five miles from Midsund. I used to go there by bicycle at night carrying the gun in my rucksack. I had to pass the torpedo station but the Germans never examined anybody there.

That season I shot eleven black-cock and one caper and considered it a good bag.

One day I heard that one of my colleagues had been arrested in Ålesund by the Gestapo. He had been examined immediately and had jumped clean through a window on the first floor and ran into a doctor's office in the neighbourhood. He had probably been tortured. The Gestapo found him there and took him away. Once more he escaped from them and tried to drown himself by jumping into the harbour. He was rescued and taken to prison. In the cell he had smashed the bulb of the electric lamp and tried to cut his veins with the pieces. I knew him as a sound and well balanced man and I can hardly believe he would try three times in a few hours to commit suicide unless he had been treated in an extraordinarily brutal way.

Well, if he was tortured I was in danger. We had met and even though both of us had used false names I knew who he was and I felt sure he knew who I was. I had to disappear. I could not take a chance. Was he arrested because of his work in the Secret Service, or could there be another reason? I asked one of my close friends to go to Ålesund and try to find out. I also told him where I would hide. I would go to Nesset and stay with Hjalmar. I would be safe there and Kristian might call me back if there was no danger.

Travel was restricted and to go by the railway I had to have a special permit from the local Sheriff. He was a good Norwegian and had lent me a hand on many occasions. I telephoned him.

"I have received orders from the Fishery Department to be in Oslo for a Conference on Thursday this week. I must leave tomorrow. There is no time to send in the usual form and await the reply. Can you send me a permit by the skipper of the Rauma tomorrow morning? Please don't send it by mail also send an application form at the same time. I'll return it immediately."

I told the teachers the same story. The next morning I smuggled my skis on board the Rauma. Nobody saw them. The skipper had my travel permission alright. In Molde I visited a friend, put on a sporting suit, left my ordinary clothes there and off I went to Åndalsnes. I bought a return ticket to Oslo and sent my skis to Otta.

I was unlucky enough to meet a former member of the council of my school on the train the next morning. I explained to him I had been called to an important meeting in Oslo, He too was going to Oslo. I managed to get a seat in another compartment but he spent more time in mine. I felt relief when he left after some time. Apparently he was not suspicious and why should he be?

At Otta I took my rucksack and alighted before the train stopped. I caught a glimpse of Mr. Farstad as he elbowed towards the canteen to get some dry sandwiches and a cup of tea substitute. I hid until the train left. Then I took my skis and made for Mysüseter. I had nearly 40 miles to travel across the mountain this time. A lorry driving timber from the valley gave me a good lift, and late in the afternoon I passed Mysüseter. There was not much snow left and I had to carry my skis for some miles but it was a wonderful night! The air was crisp and clear. The barren mountain plateau was full of small burns fed by the melting snow. The ptarmigan were calling to each other in the hills. The first birds of the spring had arrived. In front of me I had the mighty Rondane mountains, rising to 6,000 ft. I felt strong and fit for my expedition. I had no map or compass but I knew my way, and I felt happy to wander in these grand surroundings in the heart of my country. Perhaps for the last time for many years. Would I go back to Midsund or would I have to continue into Sweden? I felt an intense longing to go back home and continue my work. I felt fit for it now ... strong, healthy, nothing the matter with my nerves any more.

The sun sank behind the Rondane. Day turned into night but it was the middle of May and the night was light. A gentle, chilly breeze turned the surface of the snow into a hard crust. My skis slid easily away. At ten o'clock I had passed the watershed and at good speed I slid down the slopes towards the Atnasjø. After crossing a lake with very thin ice, I left my skis in an old *seter* barn and went on by foot. It was past midnight. I heard a black-cock playing in a big fir tree below Müvollkollen. So easy to walk. What crisp air. A woodcock passed above me. 'Psisst horrt-horrt. Psisst horrt-horrt.' I could just see the swift bird against the dark blue sky. A few pale stars were visible. I had reached the pine forest now. The fresh smell of pine needles tickled my nostrils. Ptarmigan were noisy everywhere, calling to each other, now and then bursting into loud laughter. What a night!

I would soon see the Atnasjøen lake. Would it be covered with ice yet? How could I get across? I walked on silently to see as much as possible of the animals around me. The forest, the marshes, the mountains all seemed alive with game.

Suddenly there was a man in front of me, in the twilight a hundred yards away. He carried a gun; apparently he had seen me the very moment I saw him, for he disappeared among the trees, running as fast as he could. I have never seen anyone running faster. A poacher? Who was it? Was it my friend Hjalmar whom I was going to visit? The thought amused me as it might well have been him.

The southern part of Atnasjøen was covered with ice. There was a broad, open space of water in front of me. I found a boat at Fagervoll and rowed across. Everything was silent at Nesset. No sign of life. I went up to Hjalmar's house and knocked at the door, knocked at the windows, knocked at the walls. After a while there was somebody moving, and a sleepy Inga, Hjalmar's sister, opened a window.

"It's me, Sven. Have you got a bed for me?"

"Sure, the big room in the main building. All the menfolk are out for capers tonight."

"I think I saw Hjalmar on the other side. Nobody has ever shown me such respect. He ran like a roebuck."

"Are you hungry? I have some milk and fried trout. Come inside."

Holt was there with an assistant. He was a game researcher. Both of them were out tonight to shoot caper. Ruth was there too, to assist Inga. She was an old friend of my wife and myself, and I knew she was engaged in underground work in Oslo. She was a teacher and her school had just closed until August.

It was still legal season for shooting caper. The play was at its height now, but the birds were shy and it was difficult to get near them.

Holt and his assistant had heard two last night but did not get near them. Hjalmar - I had scared him thoroughly - had heard one after he had run away from me.

They invited me to join them tonight. The best places were on the other side of the lake. There was still ice on this part of the lake but it was not strong and there was a broad open space near land on either side. We had to use a boat and a sledge. That was a new experience for me.

We set off about eleven o'clock at night. There were four of us with three guns. We towed the sledge across the open space near land, then went 'ashore' on the ice and pulled the sledge up. The next step was to hand the boat up on the sledge. Holt's assistant sat in the boat while the rest of us pulled and pushed the boat across the ice, avoiding the darkest ice which was the weakest. It was an easy job and we made good speed. Well across we pushed the sledge over the edge of the ice at the same time jumping into the boat. The edge burst and the boat floated and we rowed ashore. Hjalmar's brother Jørgen was living on this side and we went up to him. Holt and his assistant left for a place further south, Jørgen and I said we would try a place just north of the farm, Hjalmar was going to try the same bird he had heard last night.

We started at once, it was an ideal night, not too cold, not too clear. Now and then we heard and saw a woodcock passing by. Jørgen and I walked silently but with good speed. Suddenly there was a noise of whirring wings and a heavy body dashing between the trees. It was a caper. We stopped and Jørgen whispered: "Damn it, we have scared him. They don't usually sit here." Then we continued very carefully.

Jørgen stopped again after a while and made signs to me that we were close to the place. We proceeded about a hundred yards further, step by step, with the utmost care not to make the slightest noise. I carried Hjalmar's gun. He had an old one. We sat down waiting. All was quiet. A mouse was rustling around among the heather some yards away. We heard the distant rustle of a waterfall some miles up north. No wind, not the slightest noise apart from the mouse and the waterfall. Yes, there was a ptarmigan calling somewhere far up the hill.

Then suddenly there was a sharp noise as if two dry wooden sticks had been beaten together. A capercaillie. Jørgen pointed toward the direction of the noise. After a while there was another one more on the left. Two. They were sitting there for the night awaiting the first break of dawn. There was nothing more to do. There were two birds and we knew where they were sitting. They would not start playing until half-past-two or perhaps three o'clock so we slid away and spent an hour in Jørgen's cottage.

We were back again at half-past-two. It was still fairly dark but the dawn was growing slowly up north. A woodcock passed by. Suddenly the clear song of the robin cut through the silence. So tender, so clear, and so happy, and yet with a touch of sadness. Another one replied further away. In this part of the country the robin is called the 'caper clock'. Right enough, a few minutes later the caper started. This big, shy bird, averaging ten pounds in weight has the most peculiar sound of all the animals of the forest. It is impossible to describe properly because there is nothing else like it. It cannot be called a song because there is not the slightest resemblance of music or voice in it. The first phase consists of a series of noises, faintly reminding one of small dry sticks of wood being clapped together, first slowly, then in more rapid succession, and it ends in a sound like a cork being pulled out of a bottle. Then without a pause there is a sort of rhythmic hissing and creaking, and the whole thing starts again. All the time the mighty bird is wandering about on the ground or sitting on a branch in a fir tree, its huge tail spread out like a wheel, the beak raised towards the sky, the shivering wings hanging down. During the hissing the bird is quite ecstatic, blind and deaf. Therefore, as soon as the loud 'plop' has sounded and the hissing sets in you may move three or four steps towards the bird, if any slight movement apart from this is made the bird will take fright and fly.

After a few minutes the play ran quite regularly. We still listened for the other one but it had not started yet. Jørgen stayed behind, and I started moving according to the phases of the play, advancing slowly. Then the play stopped for a while and started again. The distance I had to cover did not exceed 150 yards, but the nearer I got the more careful I had to be. I also heard the second caper now. He was playing regularly, like a machine, repeating over and over the same theme. My bird was more irregular and I regretted I had not been more patient so I could have tried the other one. Anyhow, I made progress, advancing under cover of tress and small buses, every nerve alert trying not to make any uncontrolled movement. There he was. I had thought he was further away and now he was hardly 25 yards from me sitting on a branch just below the top of a tall pine. What a bird! Tail spread like a huge fan, neck stretched perpendicularly, beak half open, and a crest of beard under the bill. I could see it shivering against the bright blue sky. The play stopped before I could raise my gun. Some moments of intense excitement. Then he started again. When the 'plop' sounded, I lifted the gun to my shoulder. Bang, down came ten pounds of bird and feather rushing from one branch to another, hitting the ground with a heavy bump. The second caper flew away. Jørgen came up to me and shook my hand.

The others did not get any that night. They had heard and seen capers but had not been able to get up close enough to them. Nor did they succeed the following night. I had once promised Ruth to take her to the capers play one night and we went to a place near Nesset where we heard and saw the play at close view. A pity I had no gun that night.

I got one caper each of the following nights. Holt had two chances and got none, Hjalmar had one.

A telegram arrived for Hjalmar: 'Return barrels, tar not wanted. Opstad.'

That meant there was no apparent danger in my returning to Midsund. That my friend in Ålesund had not been arrested for suspected intelligence service work. He was arrested, but later on.

I again crossed the mountains at night, caught the train at Otta and returned from 'the important meeting in Oslo'.

I had to stay overnight at the hotel in Molde. It was full of guests but the landlady was away and I used her room. I found a radio receiver there. I did not know that Mrs. Wold was a member of the Nazi party but the radio was proof enough. She had been allowed to keep it.

Well, now I could get the news from London. The contact at the end of the leader was put inside the wardrobe, the door of which was locked but there was an electric stove in the room and I managed to connect the leader from the stove with the receiver. So next morning I tried to get London at nine o'clock. I noticed that at the back of the radio case there were more leaders than there should be. Gosh! They were connected to an extra loud speaker, probably in the hotel lounge. I praised my luck for that discovery, pulled out the contacts to the extra loud speaker and turned the screws. What joy to hear the familiar voice.

"This is the BBC. Home Service. Here is the news ..." The telephone rang.

"Hello."

"This is the office, I am sorry to bother you but Mrs. Wold will be back in half-an-hour and her room must be vacated by that time."

So I lost the news.

When I went down to the lounge half-an-hour later, my eyes fell first of all on the loud-speaker above the door. Two Nazis were sitting in the lounge!

Chapter 10

THE CRACK

Hunting black-cock and caper, crossing mountains, skiing, and also some nightly expeditions in the motor-boat to the black market had brought my physical condition to a high standard. My Secret Service work was a sport. I did not feel any danger threatening. The Gestapo might try, but they would not catch me.

My organisation warned that my colleague in Ålesund had been brought to Trondheim and was under hard pressure by the Gestapo. I ought to leave again for six weeks or two months anyway, but I stayed. In three weeks time our course would be finished. If I disappeared now it might make severe difficulties for the school. I was prepared to leave at short notice and had planned two ways of escape. By motor-boat across the North Sea, I had already sufficient fuel for such a trip. Or by foot across the mountains to Sweden. Every detail of the two routes was planned.

Our Nazi authorities prepared several difficulties for us. First they dismissed the Chairman of the School Council and replaced two of the three members with Nazis. The third member was, according to the regulations, appointed by a fishermen's organisation which was anti-Nazi and he was a good Norwegian.

All important matters concerning the school should be dealt with by the Council. As the Council's Secretary it was my duty to place matters before the Council. The new Council had been appointed from the New Year; it was now June and still there had been no meeting. I had had no contact at all with the members but I expected the Council to call me soon and I did not like the thought of it. Meanwhile I kept the former Chairman informed about everything at the school.

There was another and more sinister directive. All men of 20 to 23 years were ordered to register for compulsory 'National Labour Service'. Some of my pupils were of that age. The Home Front leaders gave orders that nobody should meet the requirement of registration. There was a more ordinary labour service too, comprising all men and women of 20. The Home Front issued the same order for them; nobody should meet that requirement either.

All over the country young men discussed the problem. Should they obey the Nazi leaders or the Home Front? In larger communities there were many of these young men. They agreed that nobody should register, and only a very few disobeyed the order of the Home Front.

Things were different in our community, there were only a few young men and they lived apart. They could not easily get together and discuss the matter. London Radio told them not to meet. It was easy enough for them to speak. They could not be punished. The boys had to take the decision all alone or very few together. France had been invaded on D-Day. Most likely the war would be over soon. Why run the risk of imprisonment and concentration camps when perhaps the other boys were registered. Norway liberated and all the Nazis thrown out before the labour service was put in action?

Registration was no doubt an act of the Nazis to get young men under control in case of an Allied invasion of Norway. Maybe the intention went further, so that the National Labour Service would mean compulsory education for Military Service on the German side.

On my return from Nesset two of my pupils came to me one night. They confessed that they had registered for National Labour Service and were frightened of the consequences. Was it right or wrong what they had done? I said it was definitely wrong. They should not have registered. I told them about the orders from the Home Front leaders and they, the Home Front, had been obeyed all over the country.

I trusted these young men. I knew their politics and knew that they were strongly anti-Nazi, they were not afraid of fighting if they were called upon. So I said: "Listen. Your final examination is taking place in a fortnight. As long as you have not completed it they can't take you away. In case they try, just leave it to me, but as soon as you have finished you are no longer under the protection of your education. Don't sleep at home, sleep on board some vessel or in a *seter* (summer farm) where only your own people know you are hiding. If they search for you, get away. Don't go across to Britain in a vessel as your family would be severely punished for that. Go to Sweden. Thousands of young men of your age will hide. The Nazis cannot punish all their parents and kinsfolk."

Then I showed them on the map how they could get from western into eastern Norway and further on to Sweden. It was my own route I showed them. I also explained to them a few places where people would help them if they mentioned my name.

Young men came to my office asking for my advice. They had received orders to meet for the National Labour Service or the ordinary labour service. Some older men came to me on behalf of their sons. They were all fishermen, most of them possessing fishing vessels or shares in fishing vessels.

We prepared documents stating that skipper N.N. had taken a young man T.T. into his service for the herring season. T.T. could not be replaced if he was taken for N.L.S. This would mean the fishing would have to be given up, or at least curtailed, and it would mean severe economical loss to N.N. The output of the fishing would be far less which again would severely affect the food situation of the country. N.N. would therefore ask the conscription authorities to desist from taking T.T. to National Labour Service for the present season.

Then I produced a statement that N.N. was an honourable man, that I knew it was true what he had written, and so on. In addition to that I 'phoned the district commissioner informing him that the conscription raised a severe economic problem to the district and would mean the loss of several hundreds of tons of valuable food to our almost starving country.

This action deprived the National Labour Service of seven or eight boys. Only one or two from our district had to go because they came to me too late. But of course they should not have gone.

The 17th June, 1944, was a Saturday. I had been working hard with one of the teachers of the school. I had been writing reports and photographing all night. Recently I had got a good series of photographs from the German batteries. Now we had finished the report and stowed everything away. I had been particularly careful during this season that all dangerous material was out of reach in case of a sudden arrest. I collected my fishing tackle and went to my *seter* in the mountains. Again I passed the torpedo station. They had just been widening the fortifications and built some new pill-boxes and they had mined a deep tunnel into the rock for the torpedo tubes. I had recent photographs of the whole station from the seaward side but they had built stores and barracks near the main road. The barracks were filled with civilian workers belonging to the organisation Todt. Most of them were German but some of them were also Dutch and French.

The birch trees had come out. Thousands of birds were singing from their crowns. The slopes of the hills were covered with primroses. There was no more snow in the mountains of the island. The mountain lakes had long been free from ice.

It was after sunset when I left the main road and found the narrow strong and deep path leading to the *seter*. The previous night I had seen the sun sink into the ocean at 11.40pm. Actually it was 10.40pm because we had one hour summer time. Although there was no night any longer in this part of the country the sun was below the horizon for a few hours and then rose again. In a few days it would be summer, the Solstice and the sun would start sinking again. A brief summer then autumn then winter again. What was lying ahead, what was hidden in the autumn and winter to come? Would the country be free again? Would our people starve? Would more of my relatives and close friends disappear in concentration camps and gaol? Would more of them be executed? What about myself? No, never! They would never get me! Even if they did I would escape. I knew the country better than the enemy and I had planned everything carefully.

There were two small lakes near my *seter*. One is shaped like a bowl, steep dark mountains rising to 2,000 ft. from its shores. This bowl is full of small dark trout. The other lake is shallow and open, situated in the mountain itself. Two years ago there were no fish living there nor had any fish ever been caught there. With some friends I had then caught a number of small trout in the lower lake, carried them up the steep hills in a pail and liberated them in the shallow lake. After three months I caught four of them again they had grown to half-a-pound each. Last autumn I caught more, this time they had grown to a pound each. This was business.

My plan now was to catch as many as possible in the lower lake and repeat the experiment. Tomorrow morning at ten I would meet a friend at the lower lake.

I had become fond of the mountains. I had had the *seter* for more than two years. The first time, Easter 1942, my wife and I had been skiing there. It took us an hour to comb the slopes from the *seter* up to

Opstadhorn, the highest point of the island 2,500 ft. above sea level. From the summit we could see the outer island belt to the west and beyond it the ocean itself. To the east we had the Molde fjord and the mighty Romsdal mountains. From the summit down to the fjord south of us was a precipice. We could see the small farms along the fjord, yes, and we could see the bottom just outside the store, greenish spots of sand mixed with brownish spots of rock and seaweed.

On the northern slope of Opstadhorn used to be a colony of mountain grouse. They were quite tame in spring time and as we ascended they would run just in front of us, with a long rolling Scottish 'Rrrrr' because we disturbed them. When we threw snowballs after them they just dived behind the big stones, then peered up again, wondering what would come next.

I used to go shooting ptarmigan in the autumn here. The mountain grouse were shy at that time. They herded in large flocks at the slopes and threw themselves out in the air long before I got within shooting range.

The *seter* itself was about half way from the fjord to the Opstadhorn, just where the old pine forest joined the barren heather-clad slopes of the mountain.

It consisted of a tiny hut and a low, longish cow stable. The walls of the hut were rough planks, the roof was corrugated iron and there was only a single window. Inside there was a sheltered entrance and a single room, about 12 by 12 ft. There was an old iron stove, a table, three stools and four berths along two of the walls. The cow stable had long ago been swept down by gales. The hut was worn and my *seter* was no beauty but the century old pine forest sheltered it. and in the crisp nights of the spring the woodcock flew whistling over it, the robin and the song thrush were singing in the forest, the ptarmigan laughing in the hills just behind the *seter,* and on calm mornings of the spring I could sometimes lie in my berth and hear the black-cock playing in the hills. After going to bed we would often lie listening to the cosy sound of fir root burning in the stove, and watching the flickering light on the old grey, unpainted walls. The wood of the walls had a grey silky tone, that was particular to old wood that had frequently been washed. The only window faced the fjord. We could see the coastal steamers and the small fishing vessels passing by there. Every day a pair of golden eagles circled in the sky above the *seter.* They had their nest only a mile west of us.

However primitive everything was up there I loved my *seter.* When I was tired from office work, of lecturing and of people, I went up there and was alone, far away from everything. I cut fat fir logs in the nearby forest, lit my fire and cooked my food there, and was happy.

18th June! It was my twelfth wedding anniversary. My wife was far away in another part of the country but we had planned to meet again shortly.

I met my friend as planned. The trout rose well to the fly and in the afternoon we carried 72 small living trout up the hills to the other lake. I know now that I will see some of them again shortly but doubted it very much in the following days.

In the evening my friend went across the hills to the northern side of the island and I went back towards Midsund. I still had something to do before I could go home. I had decided to take some pictures of the torpedo station.

I met several Germans on the road. The night was clear and pleasant, many people were out for a walk. The Germans roared and sang as usual. I have never been able to understand how they can enjoy a walk that way, when the fjord is green below the road, the birch trees are brilliant green, and the robin is singing.

At a bend of the road where nobody saw me, I left it and climbed the steep hills. Just behind the station the mountains rise up to 2,000 ft. Two or three hundred feet above the station is a settle in the rocks, with a precipice below it and another one above. The settle may be four or five hundred yards in length. This was my target. From there I would have a good view of the whole fortification. People rarely went here, and I should probably be able to photograph without being observed, even though there was no place to hide. The settle had a rich vegetation of juniper and ferns, and tall birches grew here and there.

I pressed my way through the bushes. There would be an ideal place to photograph from further on. I aimed for that point but had not thought about the crows. They had their nests in the tall birch trees and they soon fell over me with a hell of a noise. They annoyed me but I went stubbornly on. I had come so far, I would have the photographs, and I could not see the guard in his usual place down at the station. I tried to behave well so as to convince the crows that

127

I would not rob their nests when I suddenly ran into three or four sheep which had been hidden by the bushes. Of course they started running and bleating, they stopped when I stopped, ran and bleated again as soon as I tried to move on.

However I had come to the ideal spot and there was still no guard to be seen, so I took off my rucksack and sat down for a while in the vain hope that the crows would get tired of screaming and the sheep of bleating. Neither of them did. The noise just went on and on. I went to work. I found the camera and the light meter in my rucksack. It was just ten o'clock. I took eight or nine pictures, some of them with the telescopic lens, and noted the particulars about time, aperture, distance and target on a piece of paper. I had a very good view of the station, so I felt quite sure I had secured some good shots.

I had to go on for about two hundred yards to find my way down from the settle. The crows and the sheep were not so bad any more, and I felt quite happy, when I suddenly noticed two or three soldiers running full speed out of the station, gun in hand, steel helmets on their heads. More came after, soon there were about 15 of them running towards the hills, yes, towards me, and spreading fan-wise so as to surround me.

I had been observed, there was no doubt about that, and now the point was to make the best possible out of the situation. I proceeded as if my conscience was perfectly clear. When I passed a big stone, I took off my rucksack and took the camera and the equipment belonging to it, including the paper with the notes. There was a hole under the stone. I put everything down there, covered it with heather and tried to make the place look natural. I went on towards the slope where I could crouch down. I heard the soldiers breaking their way through the bushes not far away, and I heard them shouting to each other, but I could not see them any more.

I found my slope alright and slid down, and started crossing the moor below. I had passed through the ring of soldiers, but they would probably soon see me here.

Suddenly a shot was fired behind me. The bullet threw some earth in the air just in front of me and a voice roared: "Halt!"

I surrendered unconditionally.

Chapter 11

EVENTS UNFOLD

"What is the matter? Why do you shout? What does this mean?"

"You are supposed to be a spy. My orders are to take you to the torpedo station."

"Are you sure you have not captured the wrong person?"

"I have my orders, you will be able to explain to the C-in-C."

"That is alright. It will soon be cleared up. A lovely night, isn't it?"

He looked at me concerned but did not reply. We walked down to the station. Near the entrance was a crowd of civilian and Todt Germans. I tried to look cheerful, but I don't think I quite succeeded.

The C-in-C was a young lieutenant. I said: "I have been arrested, Herr Leutnant, and my guard says I am supposed to be a spy. Will you please explain what all this means?"

"The guard says he watched you photographing from the settle up there and it is my duty to keep you under arrest until the case has been examined."

I told him my name and my position, and said I had been to the mountains for the weekend. It was quite correct I had been to the settle, but I had a particular reason for being there.

"As you will know, I am a zoologist, and this is the only place where the crows nest. Some years ago I had a tame crow which I had captured when young, and it was the most amusing bird you can imagine. Tonight I went up there to try to find a new one to tame."

"It is true that you have not taken pictures up there?"

"Of course not. I have not even got a camera. My camera is at home and I have got no film for it."

"Well, Herr Direktor, I am convinced this is a misunderstanding, and I am very sorry to have put you in this disagreeable position but you must understand that I have had to take these steps when the guard reported he has seen you taking photographs. As soon as we have performed the necessary examinations you will of course be released."

"I quite understand, Herr Leutnant, it is your duty, and of course I am at your disposal as long as you find it necessary."

"May I examine your rucksack?"

"Certainly," and I took out everything, there was no camera.

"Have you hidden anything on the settle?"

"No."

"The guard says he saw you hiding something under a big stone up there."

"No, as far as I remember I took my rucksack off there for a moment to put on my jacket, because it was getting chilly."

I did not like the situation.

The Lieutenant repeated his apologies for keeping me, and said I would be released as soon as the soldiers had come back.

"It is alright Leutnant, I am just as interested as you are to see everything cleared up but I am tired and thirsty because I have been walking in the mountains all day. May I have a glass of water please.

I was terribly thirsty, that was true. I always get thirsty when I am frightened, and I was frightened now.

"Would you like a cup of coffee?"

A few minutes later I had a cup of genuine coffee in my hands. Norwegians had their last coffee ration just before Christmas 1942 but I was too scared to make any remark about that. I tried another theme:

"We have spoken together by telephone before, Herr Leutnant, can you remember that?"

"I am sorry, no."

"It was about a year ago. Your people came with a lorry to my school and took away several tons of stones which we had there and intended to use for levelling the courtyard. I rang you up and you promised that the stones would be brought back."

"Oh yes, now I remember."

"We never got the stones back. I suppose your promise is still valid and that we will get them back soon?"

"I am sorry for that, Herr Direktor, I thought you had them back long ago. I'll see that they are brought up tomorrow."

The soldiers began to return, six or seven of them were back now. All of them saluted the Lieutenant and reported that nothing had been found. I kept looking at each of them as they came in, waiting to see if my camera was brought before the Lieutenant.

"Well, Herr Direktor, I am so sorry to keep you so long, I am convinced the whole thing has been cleared up, and I can see no reason to keep you here any longer."

"To be quite honest, Herr Leutnant, there is a reason why I really want to get home before midnight. Our final examination is going to start tomorrow morning. We expect a censor to arrive from Molde with the Åndalsnes steamer at about three o'clock in the morning. As you may know it is not stopping at Midsund so I will have to go out in a motorboat and stop the steamer in the fjord. The engine has not been used for sometime so I want to look it over before I go out. If you find it necessary to ask me some further questions later on, you know where I live, and I will be at your disposal at any time."

I was free again but still some soldiers were out searching for my camera. The Lieutenant had told me where it was. I was quite sure they would find it within the hour. Things would be serious then.

I passed the camp and started on my road to Midsund. Soldiers were still coming down the slopes. I looked at them and tried to find out if one of them had my camera but I could not see clearly.

However, I was quite sure the camera would soon be found, certainly my time was very limited. As soon as I was out of sight I speeded up. On my arrival at Midsund I did not go home at once but left my rucksack at the boat-house and then went home.

Mrs. Voile met me in the hall: "You must be hungry, come and have something to eat."

I was awfully hungry but was too busy to eat so I replied:

"Thank you, I have just had a substantial meal and I'll have to see that the engine on board the 'Laks' is in order. You know the Censor is coming tonight?"

I had become an expert and clever liar now.

I went upstairs. Captain Roald met me: "The first Censor has arrived and he would appreciate seeing you."

I had to see him and wasted some valuable time in being polite.

Then I called Mr. Johannsen. "I have been arrested. I will certainly be rearrested within 30 minutes or an hour. You know what it means. I must try and get across to England in the Laks. Will you please go to the school at once. Take the small compass, a North Sea chart, a drift anchor, a long rope and my oilskin coat and trousers. Bring them to the pier. Go to Kristian and get a barrel of oil, ten gallons of lubricating oil, food and water for a week and have everything ready there in half-an-hour. All our secret things have been stowed away. You know where they are. The last films are there. Send them to headquarters as soon as everything here is quiet. Go away into hiding if they catch me again. Send the following cable to my wife at once: 'Send the attestation to Gertie.' It means: 'Go to Sweden at once'. Then there is another thing the Censor is coming tonight with the Åndalsnes steamer to act as censor here. You must fetch him. Arrange to borrow a motorboat, Olav-on-the-Telefone has probably got one. Can you remember all this? I must clean the filter to the motor. I'll be at the pier in half-an-hour."

Johannsen went off to collect the things and I went on board the Laks taking my rucksack with me. There was a sleeping bag, a jersey and some other useful things in it.

There was a lot of water in the boat and I had to pump

for at least ten minutes before it was empty. Then I took the filter apart and cleared it. The engine would have to run continuously for two or three days and I did not want an unexpected stop. Then I started it. It was a new diesel engine and it ran smoothly.

I was at the pier in good time. Nothing was ready. Kristian was there and said: "Sorry to hear you have been in trouble. Come and have a drink and let us talk things over."

"No, I must go to England at once. Have you got everything here? We must get it on board at once."

Just then Johannsen came running round the corner: "The Germans are in Voile's house. They may be here any moment."

I ran to the boat.

"I'll get everything in the outer islands. Goodbye."

And off I went at full speed heading for the nearest little island where I would be out of sight of the Germans until I was out of reach of their guns. I was hardly 50 yards away when a shot was fired. The bullet hit the sea just beside me. They had a machine gun at the pier already. No chance at all to escape. Laks was an open boat.

I surrendered unconditionally for the second time. It was midnight and it was the end of my twelfth wedding anniversary.

Chapter 12

UNDER ARREST

The Lieutenant himself had fired the shot. There he was at the pier with a Bren gun and a steel helmet.

"You are under arrest for attempting to escape."

"I have not tried to escape."

"Where were you going in the motor-boat?"

"My dear Leutnant, when I left you an hour ago, I told you I was going to look after the motor-boat. I have been refuelling here and was on my way back to the buoy."

"You did not stop when we shouted."

"I heard no shouting. I was sitting close to a noisy engine. You cannot expect me to hear shouting at a distance."

"You have lied to me. I am very disappointed. We have found the camera. If you had told me at once we might have arranged the affair between ourselves. Now it has been my duty to send for the Military Police. They will take you to Molde in about two hours."

"Of course I lied. What would you have done in similar circumstances?"

He did not reply. I continued: "This affair could not have been arranged between ourselves if you had done your duty."

"You are telling me you are not trying to escape in the motor-boat. Why have you got your rucksack and your sleeping bag on board?"

"It is the same outfit as I had in the torpedo station an hour ago. I went directly on board when I left you to bring the engine in order to refuel. Furthermore I thought I might sleep on board the boat for an hour or two until the Åndalsnes steamer arrived. If I went home to sleep I would lose time and perhaps even oversleep."

The Lieutenant set another soldier with another Bren gun to search my pockets for weapons. Then I was placed in a lorry just behind the steering house. The Lieutenant climbed up beside the driver. One soldier placed himself opposite me with a pistol, another one with a Bren gun pointing at me, two more soldiers seated themselves in the two rear corners, each of them with a Bren gun pointing at me, and off we went. I was first taken home where the Lieutenant informed me I would be allowed to take my shaving set, one set of underwear, and one set of pyjamas with me. I would probably never return here again. Mrs. Voile was called for. She brought me the things and off we went again.

Several of the pupils and the villagers were out walking, enjoying the bright night and fine weather.

I knew all of them and waved to them as we passed. My guard shouted: "Stop that or we shoot!"

I looked at them one by one and said: "You guard me well. This is what we call in Norway spreading butter on pork."

"Hold your tongue or we shoot!"

I had a pack of American cigarettes in my pocket. My sister, who was in Sweden had sent it to me by illegal means. Nobody should know she was in Sweden and it would be difficult to explain how I had got them. Of course they would be used against me as proof that I was a spy and had connections with the 'enemy', I wanted to get rid of them but I was too well guarded to throw them away. So I smoked as many as I could until we arrived in the torpedo station.

I was taken to the Officers' Mess. It had double windows and one door. The Lieutenant came to examine me and brought with him my camera and the outfit that they had found under the big stone.

"Are these things yours?"

"Yes."

"So you have taken pictures from up there?"

"Yes."

"Do you know it is strictly prohibited?"

"Yes, that is why I hid the camera."

"Why did you take those pictures? Are you working for London?"

"No Herr Leutnant, as I told you, I went up to that settle in order to catch a young crow. I have never been up there before and I was surprised to see all these buildings you have built here and have altered the once so peaceful meadows belonging to Rasmu's farm. As I had my camera in my rucksack I thought it would be a most interesting picture to have after the war, when everything goes back to normal and the building here are removed. So without any further thought at all I took the pictures.

Then I saw your soldiers coming out from the station, I remembered that photographing of German barracks and the like is strictly forbidden. If the camera was found and the pictures developed I might be taken for a spy. That means the death penalty. My thought was to hide the camera at any price, and that is why I hid it."

"But, Herr Direktor, that was the most foolish thing you could do. Your position is very grave now."

"Yes, I admit it was foolish. But in hiding the camera I had a chance of escaping the penalty. If you found the camera my only chance was that you would believe me."

"But you took more than one picture. Your list comprises nine photographs."

"Yes that is right. But remember I am an amateur photographer. It was late at night and difficult light conditions. I always take a series of pictures under such circumstances. If you develop the film, you will find that earlier in the day I took some pictures of trout in the mountains you will notice that also on that occasion I took more than one picture."

"I am afraid the Military Police will not believe your story. I don't understand how you could do such a foolish thing."

He was right, of course, I had been careless and I had been captured and that was that.

The Lieutenant left me and a guard with a Bren gun was placed on the door, given orders to guard me well and keep aiming with the gun at me all the time. There was a bench near the window. I packed up my sleeping bag and sat down on it. I had the problem of the American cigarettes to solve.

I picked out the cigarettes one by one, tore the paper off them and put the tobacco in my tobacco purse, curling the paper and dropping the small paper pellets on the floor. At last I had destroyed all of them, but I still had the cover left. I made a pellet of that too, yawned and stretched out both my arms as if I were mighty sleepy, and hid the cover behind a blind. I was quite satisfied at that manoeuvre, maybe when the nights became dark they would use the blinds again and find the cover and suspect that one of the Germans had had connections with the enemy. So I crept into my sleeping bag and tried to sleep.

The guard spoke to me in a low voice:

"*Schade*" he said

"Yes," I said, "It is schade."

Schade is the German word for pitiful.

"No, no," he said. "I mean my name is Shade. You are in a very dangerous position," he added, "I am afraid you will be shot. How could you do such a foolish thing?"

I admitted I had been very foolish.

"Do you know Olaf?" he asked.

"Do you mean Olaf-in-the-Meadow?"

"Yes, we drank a bottle of liqueur together last night."

"I don't understand how my countrymen can fraternise with German soldiers that way."

"I am not German, I am Hungarian."

"But you are in German uniform and in the service of the Germans. Imagine if Hungary was occupied by Russians and Poles, would you like your countrymen to drink with the Poles?"

"No, but that is something different."

"No, it is exactly the same."

"I don't mind who wins the war. The Germans will lose it. I don't mind who will occupy my country: English, American, even the French. Only not the Russians. Only not the Russians."

142

"Why not the Russians? They are not as bad as you think. You have been filled with propaganda against them. Can you remember the beginning of the war? Do you remember the Pact of Friendship between Germany and Russia? Do you remember Hitler said that National Socialism and Communism were closely related to each other. That the friendship between Germany and Russia was not to last for a year or two but for thousands of years, for ever! And now, Bolshevism is the destructive, National Socialism the constructive idea. Can't you see that it is all propaganda?"

"The Russians are barbarians."

"Hitler did not say that in August 1939."

Our discussion was interrupted. The Military Police had arrived in their vessel. Two of them entered the room. They had steel helmets, pistols and a chain around the neck. The chain carried a metal plate with the inscription: Feldgendamerie.

One of the sergeants roared across the table to me: "Get up, so you are the swine of a spy?"

"I am no spy."

"*Halt's Maul!* Shut up, follow us. Hurry up."

We went into the office. The Lieutenant was there.

The Sergeant roared again: "Hands up! Turn round!"

They searched my pockets carefully, placing the contents on the table.

The Sergeant was a tall, well-built fellow, with a brutal face, a flat broken nose and a disagreeable hoarse voice. A typical representative of the *Herrenvolk*. His companion did not look quite so unpleasant, but he too looked brutal.

The Sergeant took up a notebook and started examining me. As he mostly spoke through his nose, I did not understand a word he was saying; he spoke very fast as well.

I told him I did not understand. He just raised his voice and roared. I had to ask again. Then he got furious, sprang to his feet, banged the table, and roared. The Lieutenant tried to interfere. I said, "If you will speak slowly and distinctly, and not so loudly, I will do my best to reply to everything. I have nothing to hide."

I suppose the presence of the Lieutenant calmed him. He looked angry for a moment, then pulled himself together and started asking questions slowly and distinctly. He asked almost the same questions as the Lieutenant had done. I gave him the same explanations.

Suddenly he roared again, "You are a damned spy! There is not a word of truth in what you are telling me. We know how to handle people like you. Now will you tell the truth? It is much better to tell it at once. Just get it out."

"I have told the truth. I admit it may sound strange to you. I also admit I have done silly things but most people at sometime or other do silly things. When I took those pictures, it was not in my mind that it was prohibited. I only thought of that when I saw the soldiers coming towards me."

"And where did you intend to go in your motor-boat? It was an attempt to escape. So you invented the story about the Censor. Ha, ha, ha. But we will have the pleasure of fetching your Censor. We'll go out and see his arrival and you will come with us." "I am confident he will come."

"Afterwards you will be taken to prison and tried. Nobody, nobody, will believe your stories. You will be shot as a spy."

Both the MPs drew their pistols. I was ordered to get up. The Lieutenant looked sorry but he said nothing. I was escorted to the vessel. It was an ordinary fishing vessel, some 50 ft. long with a machine-gun mounted on the front deck. The crew consisted of four ratings. We set off. I sat down on the hatch. The MPs guarded me one on each side.

On the fjord off Midsund there was another motor-boat waiting: Olaf on the telephone with Mr. Johannsen. The Sergeant asked me: "Who are they?"

"One of our teachers, Mr. Johannsen, to fetch the Censor." We went up to them.

"Tell him we will fetch the Censor. Tell him to moor at our side and to stand by."

I did so and added, "Take the code book away."

The code book was the only thing I had not hidden properly. It was an ordinary book among other ordinary books in my library but there were some small pencil marks on some of the pages and I felt it would be safer to get the book away.

The steamer approached. It was late, nearly five o'clock in the morning. The Sergeant shouted to two of the ratings: "Stand by the machine-gun."

The ratings took off the cover and made it clear. It was ridiculous, the steamer would stop if anyone waved and even if they just saw a boat waiting.

The steamer was quite near now, again the Sergeant shouted: "Aim at the bow."

The skipper of the ship was apparently irritated at these preparations. He did not stop until the very last moment.

The sergeant called out to me: "Do you see the Censor?"

This was ridiculous as it was impossible at such a distance to recognise anybody on deck.

"Not yet."

When the steamer was quite near I saw the harbour master from Molde entering the deck, suitcase in hand.

"There he is."

The Sergeant looked disappointed. The Censor was really there. That part of my story was not a lie anyway.

Then he brightened up. "Ah-ha, so he is your Molde connection. He belongs to the organisation!"

146

"Sorry, Herr Sergeant, I don't know of any organisation. I have only seen him once before and that was a year ago, when he was a Censor at our school. The books at the school will prove that."

The harbour master entered our vessel and looked bewildered. I said: "Welcome to Midsund. Don't speak to me, I am a prisoner."

"Don't speak together," shouted the Sergeant.

We went to Midsund. The whole party was silent. Then the Sergeant said to me: "We are going to search your home. You must show us the way."

We landed at Oppstad's pier. I had a rating on either side, an M.P. in front of me and one behind. It was a safe escort, although I cannot remember if the ratings carried arms.

One of my former pupils passed us on our way to Voile's house. I nodded to him and he twinkled with his eyes in reply.

Immediately the Sergeant, who was in front of me shouted, to the M.P. behind: "Arrest him!"

Poor Hans was suddenly seized by three strong men. He carried a small rucksack.

The Sergeant asked me: "Do you know him?"

"Yes, he was one of my former pupils."

Then he ordered the men to examine the rucksack. The contents were spread in the middle of the road:

some coloured scarves, some lacquered belts and a mirror or two. Hans had obviously been away to see a girlfriend somewhere and had been rebuffed so had to bring his gifts home again.

"*Du bist entlassen.*"

Hans looked bewildered at me. I had to translate: "You are free."

His face lit up in a broad smile, he collected his things and disappeared.

Mrs. Voile met us as we entered the house. There was a trace of tears in her eyes. She asked the guards: "Can he have breakfast here before you take him away?"

I had to translate.

"Yes if you have everything ready, we are short of time."

Again I translated and added to console her. "Take it easy. It's alright, I'll soon be free again."

I believed it myself, I had made up my mind to try any possibility of escaping.

Upstairs in my own room the Germans at once set to examine all my belongings. They emptied the wardrobes, the drawers of my writing desk and looked over my books. Meanwhile, I was allowed to change my sporting suit for an ordinary one and to wash thoroughly. I had to explain everything they found but they did not find much of interest.

One of the ratings took a special interest in my bookshelves. He found literature about Germany first of all. There was Hitler's *Mein Kampf.*

The Sergeant asked: "Have you read it?"

"Yes of course."

"And yet you are a Jøssing!"

(Jøssing is a Norwegain anti-Nazi, the antagonist of the Quisling)

They found Rausching's *Hitler Speaks*; they also found Ragnar Wold's *Germany is Marching.* I translated and to the latter I had the pleasure of adding the subtitle: "Why and where to?"

They collected everything that might look suspicious on a table together with the camera and all the small things they had found in my pockets at the torpedo station.

I said: "Will I be allowed to smoke during the next few days?"

"Yes, certainly."

"Then I suppose I may take my tobacco and my cigarettes away with me."

"Certainly."

The Sergeant went to the telephone station to telephone meanwhile the other M.P. guarded me outside. The ratings had gone on board. The Sergeant had calmed down and was no longer rude to me. Apparently he had started to regard me as an innocent and quiet prisoner, I decided to behave exemplarily - until the right moment which I felt sure would come.

Kristian Opstad came along to keep me company. He asked me: "Have you enough tobacco?"

"Yes thank you."

The M.P. interrupted: "You are not allowed to speak to the prisoner."

Kristian did not pay him any attention. "I'll bring you some packs of cigarettes if you want them."

"No thank you, I have sufficient. As soon as I get into prison I am not allowed to smoke."

"You must not speak together."

Kristian went on: "I'll inform your wife and Professor Dahl. I don't mind this damned German, he cannot prevent me from speaking. We will take care of your things. Our country will soon be free again."

The Sergeant came back. I had seen faces in the windows of the nearest houses. People came out now and we shook hands. There was the midwife, dear old Ingeborg-at-the-telephone, Mrs. Opstad and some others. They went down to the pier and waved to me as we set off. All of them looked sad. Ingeborg shed some tears in her apron.

Again I was sitting on the hatch. It was chilly and I had my coat on. I could put my hands through the pockets and I held the matchbox in my jacket. I was closely guarded all the time but I managed to empty the file of tablets and to put some loose tablets into each of the pockets of my suit. The tablets being very small would probably not be found there even if I was searched once more. Then I lit up my pipe with a match, nobody noticed when I threw the match overboard with the empty glass tube.

There was a puppy dog on board which evidently belonged to the ratings. One of them called for it. The puppy started howling and ran up to me, crawling into my legs, trying to hide. The rating took it away and beat it soundly. I thought: 'Just the same way as they make friends with the Norwegians'.

They took it down to the cabin. I heard the puppy howling and the rating beating it for a long time. Then suddenly the puppy was on deck again, creeping, still whining, into my lap.

I had seen a similar case before. A year ago they had a young dog at the torpedo station. One day it came running to Midsund and scratched at Jørgen's door. The Germans fetched it back on the following day. Some days later it was there again and this time it was allowed to stay, but it became terrified whenever any Germans passed by and crept into hiding.

The Germans used to tell us they loved animals and children!

We arrived in Molde at about 9.00am. I had slept during the latter part of the journey. Now the M.Ps escorted me through the main streets of Molde. There were still ruins on both sides of the street after the bombing in 1940, but a number of barracks had been built to provide lodging for shops.

We passed one of my colleagues in the Secret Service. I nodded towards my guards and was pleased to see he noticed it. Now he would know there was danger and he would no doubt warn the others.

The M.P. Headquarters were in a dairy building. I was taken to the M.P. chief. He was a tall, dark, distinguished looking officer, aged about 40. Later on I learned that he was a Gestapo chief from Alesund. He spoke distinctly and had an agreeable voice. His questions were brief and clear.

"Do you speak German?"

"Yes."

"Do you want an interpreter?"

"No."

He took my name and particulars. A young and very pretty office girl wrote everything down in shorthand. He asked the names of my wife, my mother, my brothers and sisters and their addresses. I gave all of those who had my own surname, but not my married sisters and their husbands, because I knew that every Sømme would be checked anyway. The others probably not.

"Your pocket book please."

I handed it over. It contained a fair sum of money. I had this with me as I had been prepared to go into hiding and might need it. The money was put into an envelope and put aside.

"Are you a relative of Iacob Sømme?"

"He was my brother."

"He was shot because he was a spy. That is very bad for your case."

"No, the newspapers said he was shot because he had placed his knowledge and abilities in the service of the enemy."

"What was his special knowledge?"

"He was a zoologist."

"And you are a zoologist too?"

"Yes."

"It is very remarkable. You are brothers. You are both zoologists. You were both arrested for the same crime. I suppose you very often wrote to each other?"

"No, very rarely. It is more than two years since I last heard from him, and that was, I think, the only letter for more than a year."

"Were you often in Oslo?"

"When I was ordered to Oslo by my Ministry, twice or three times a year."

"You were educated, both of you as zoologists. Is your

wife University educated too?"

"Yes."

"Zoologist?"

"Yes."

"And your brother's wife?"

"Yes."

"And your second brother?"

"Yes."

"Zoologist?"

"No, he is a civil engineer."

He raised his voice in anger: "Damn it, you Norwegians all seem to be educated, even the son of a poor fisherman is getting an education."

"That is right, in our Fishery School."

"And now to your explanation. It is untrue, it is childish to think we will believe it."

"Nevertheless it is true."

"You cannot maintain it at the court-martial. They will get the truth out of you and this is going to cost you your head."

I did not reply.

"Do you understand what I told you? You are going to be shot. Is that clear?"

"Quite, only I feel it is a bit harsh for taking some pictures for post-war pleasure."

I was escorted back through the main street again and taken to a German naval prison in a barrack. A hundred yards away was once my parents' home where I spent six happy years of my boyhood until my father had died and we moved to Eastern Norway. The house was still there but the tuberculosis hospital where my father was a house surgeon was bombed and burnt down in 1940. The only part that was saved was the children's department. The Germans had built their naval headquarters all around the remains of the hospital to obtain the protection of its Red Cross.

As I had expected, my tobacco and all that was left in my pockets including my watch was taken away from me, four hours after they had told me I would be allowed to smoke. By special permission, they informed me, I would be allowed to keep my wedding ring. They also kept my braces, lest I should hang myself. I was pleased they did not find my small tablets.

My new guard was a jovial fellow in his fifties, with a reddish face and a good round stomach. Apparently I was the only prisoner. My guard told me that whenever I wanted something I could just press the bell. He offered me coffee. There was an enormous mug of surrogate lukewarm coffee in a mug on the radiator in the corridor. I was allowed to walk out for it myself.

155

My cell was about 8ft by 6ft wide with a wooden bench, a small table nailed to the wall and a stool. Then there were the regulations. When the Inspector or some officer arrived I would have to stand up close to the window and salute, saying for instance: 'Prisoner number six, charged with seven days imprisonment for such and such offence.'

The bench was bare. My guard told me I would get a blanket at 7.00pm.

I slept away most of the day. I decided to sleep and rest when I had no chance of escape, and to be wide awake whenever the slightest chance occurred. At 2.00pm my guard brought me a large portion of pea soup with pieces of meat in it. Indeed, better food than most Norwegians had. I had a loaf of bread, a small lump of butter and a piece of cheese.

It was a long day. I found two pieces of string in a pocket and tried to remember how to form a wall knot and how to crown it. After several attempts I succeeded. Then I spliced the strings together, one long splice, one short. Afterwards I tried some gymnastics. I thought how horrible imprisonment must be for all my thousands of countrymen who were put into solitary or dark cells for weeks, months and years, who were tortured and beaten, humiliated by inhuman guards every day for years. I praised my good fortune that I had been handled only by soldiers so far, and was going to be court-martialled instead of being left with the Gestapo for torture and 60-hour examinations. Correct treatment, sentence and a quick end was a fate indeed far better than any kind of Gestapo treatment. I did not know then that it had become the custom in similar cases to leave the prisoner to a treatment by the Gestapo before the trial.

At 7.00pm I was taken to the guards' room where my M.P. guard from the previous night, not the Sergeant, but the better tempered one, with his steel helmet and his chain around his neck and the plate on his chest, waited. He told me he would be taking me to Dombas, 80 or 90 miles inland by railway from Åndalsnes. I knew there was a military headquarters up there. I was given back my watch, a box of matches and some coins they had found in my pockets when I entered the prison. I also had my loaf of bread and Mrs. Voile's sandwiches as provisions for the journey, and my briefcase containing underwear and my toilet articles. Before we left my M.P. guard took up handcuffs and chained my right arm to his left. Thus we walked to the quay. We were to go by the local steamer *Hankø* to Åndalsnes, stay on board there, and take the Oslo express train to Dombas at 8.00am next morning.

The steamer was late and we had to wait for it on the quay. I was glad of that because it gave me an opportunity to show my handcuffs to some people I knew and who were also waiting for the steamer. Among them were Mrs. Hole, widow of the former Sheriff at Gossen and Mrs. Moe, an old friend of my family. I learnt that this exhibition of my humiliation had had some effect and that my collaborators in the Secret Service in Molde had sent two men with the *Hankø* to try and rescue me. I am sorry I disappointed them.

Chapter 13

THE ESCAPE

We had a first class cabin in the bottom of the ship. There were two berths opposite each other, and a small locker and a bull's eye above that. My guard freed himself of the handcuff. Instead, my wrists were linked together under my right knee. I moaned as he did it, although it did not hurt, and he loosened it. Then he left me without locking the door. My left handcuff was loose. I tried to see if it would be possible to slip it over my hand and discovered that it was wide enough, provided I used spit. Then I examined the bull's eye and found it sufficiently wide to allow me to creep through it. I tried to judge my chances of escape and decided they were not bright. I might get off one handcuff and slip out of the bull's eye, swim round the steamer and get unseen ashore under the poles of the wooden pier. But lots of people would see me crossing the main street and my escape would be discovered by my guard as well within a few minutes. No, my prospects were poor at the moment. I decided to wait for a better chance.

As soon as my guard came back I asked him to get me something to drink because I was thirsty. He went to the waitress and came back with a bottle of beer but no glass. I drank from the bottle and had to lift my knee above my head. An awkward position for drinking.

Afterwards I fell asleep, sitting on the edge of the berth, my guard sitting opposite me. After a while he awakened me, opened the small door of the locker and said I would be more comfortable if I put my feet on the door. I asked him to take off my shoes, so I could sit on the end of the berth, back against the wall, and he did so. Again I fell asleep and again he woke me, saying: "I'll take off your handcuffs so that you may stretch and sleep." He even covered me with my coat and I fell asleep for the third time, lying conveniently on the berth.

I was awoken by the slamming of the cabin door. Evidently the mate had opened it to look for something.. The monotonous strokes of the engine had ceased. Our cabin was dark now because the bull's eye turned to a pier. Probably Åndalsnes.

Opposite me, sitting on the edge of his berth, was my guard, asleep, his chin resting on his breast. No wonder. He had told me that this was his third night in succession on duty. Last night he had been taking me from Midsund to Molde.

This situation appeared to me as a possibility of escape. I summed up my chances. The cabin door was not locked. The crew and the passengers were Norwegians and would hardly stop me. I wore civilian clothes. The only thing was that my guard might awake when I left the door and I did not relish the thought of being shot going through the door. I put on my shoes. Then to test if my guard was sound asleep I said: "I must get out."

He did not stir. I repeated it still louder.

"I must get out!"

I made up my mind to take nothing with me. My briefcase with underwear and toilet articles would not be necessary and might raise suspicion if I had to pass a guard on the quay. My coat would hamper me. I could do without it. But food was essential. I took the loaf of bread and Mrs. Voile's sandwiches out of my briefcase and unpacked the sandwiches to see if the noise of the paper would awaken my guard but he just went on sleeping. I don't know why, but perhaps from nervousness I took a big mouthful of one of the sandwiches, then wrapped them up and put them in my pocket. I put the bread under my jacket and put on my hat. I looked for my guard's pistol. It might be useful, but he had slumped down over it so I could not get it without awakening him. Then stealthily I slid out of the cabin and closed the door carefully behind me.

I went up the stairs leading to the deck entrances. Both the doors were locked. I was trapped.

There was a ladies' compartment in front of me. I opened the door. Eight women were sleeping there. I examined the windows; they were all screwed into the frames. Opposite the ladies' compartment was one for gentlemen. It was full of them. One of them was awake. I whispered to him: "The air is very bad here, isn't it possible to open a window?"

"It is so hot and uncomfortable here, but all the windows are screwed into the frames."

There was apparently nothing to do but go back down to my guard again. I went down the stairs and already had my hand on the door handle, when a thought struck me. There was a corridor leading under the deck to the front of the ship. I started walking forwards. Near the front end of the corridor there were some people talking together. To avoid passing them I went across the top of the engine room, thinking there would be a similar corridor on the other side. But when I opened the door, it was the chief engineer's cabin and the chief received me with language that would be indecent to repeat here. I don't blame him as he had probably just fallen asleep.

Well, that was that, I had to pass the people in the corridor. There was a staircase leading to the foredeck.

The mate was at the winch, unloading the wares that were to be sent on the train later in the morning. On the pier, just where I had to go ashore, there was a German sentry with his gun.

Nothing but impudence can do it, I thought, and with a 'Cheerio' as happy as I could produce it, I waved to the mate and stepped ashore beside the sentry. The mate gave me a broad smile and went on unloading. The sentry did not stir. I was afraid he would stop me to see what I was hiding under my jacket. My loaf of bread was there. I looked at my watch, it was 2.15am.

The railway blocked my way to Isfjorden, where I intended to go. I had to pass the railway station, where there was another sentry, some German barracks with a third sentry, the bridge over the rails with a fourth and the locomotive yard with a fifth sentry. I tried to walk as quietly and naturally as I could. Then I discovered that I was still chewing the mouthful of sandwich which I had taken in the cabin when I left my guard there. I had been too excited to swallow it. I now made a conscious effort to do so but mouth was so dry I was unable to and had to spit it out.

I did not dare to go to Romsdal. It was a narrow valley, the mountains rising to five or six thousand feet on either side. The main road and the railway to Oslo are running there, and there were many German camps along it. My plan was to head for one of the Isfjord valleys and try to get across the mountains to the Eikesdal valley. Then I could follow my old planned route into eastern Norway across the Dovre Mountains and further into Sweden. As I did not know the Isfjord valleys intimately it might be a difficult and hazardous walk. If it proved to be too difficult I might turn North and get into the Langfjord district.

I took the Isfjord road, passing the long street through Åndalsnes. I felt an urge to run but did not dare as I might be observed and halted by the Germans. It was just as well I resisted because there was a camp with Russian PoWs close to the road where a prisoner was talking with the guard as I passed it and as far as they could see I was walking normally.

I calculated my guard on board the ship might sleep for at least half-an-hour, perhaps even two hours, then he would awake, give the alarm, and every soldier in Åndalsnes would be sent out in search of me. They would send cars along the roads and they would certainly use bloodhounds. My coat and briefcase were left on board the steamer. They would let the hounds sniff them first.

Therefore as soon as I had passed all houses and was well out of sight of the sentry at the prison camp I started running. I had the fjord on my left side, a steep slope on my right. Small streams were coming down the mountains because there was still much snow higher up.

Suddenly I jumped from the middle of the road sideways into one of the small streams and started climbing the slope. The hounds could not trace any scent in the stream. For one or two hours I walked along smaller and bigger burns, mostly upstream, towards the mountains, also passing ditches alongside the hills, and sometimes walking downstream.

Every now and then I listened but nothing could be heard except the rushing sound of all the small burns and the birds which had started singing.

It was a lovely morning. The mountainside was covered with birch trees, bird-cherries and alders. The leaves had just come out and the moist air was filled with the sweet scent of spring. Song-thrush and robins were singing and cuckoos calling everywhere. I felt strong and fit for the task ahead of me and felt sure the Germans would never again catch me. Suddenly there came over me a strong sense of freedom and joy. I had escaped torture, imprisonment and death, I was free like the birds singing around me. There was no school any more, no more responsibility, no property to take care of. Life was ahead of me. I was an outlaw. Everything now was up to me. I could sing with joy, I was free, free, free.

The loaf of bread under my arm hampered my movements. I had no knife and it was too hard to break so I picked up a stone and smashed the loaf to pieces and put the pieces in my pockets. I had my watch, a box of matches and Kr1.50. That was all.

After a while I met with the first spots of snow and avoided them. I did not want to leave tracks. In one place I met a long, narrow, continuous strip of snow. To avoid going round it I climbed across it from tree to tree like an ape, if not quite as graceful. Later I came down to a green valley. The mountains round it were hidden in the mist, so I could not see where it led to but thought it might lead to the Eikesdal Valley. There was a narrow road on my side of the river. As I crossed it I studied every mark on it carefully. Nobody seemed to have walked or driven there today but I was not quite sure. I decided to walk up this valley and try to get across to the Eikesdal Valley. I would walk the far side of the valley where the Germans would not trace me so easily. Several times I tried to cross the river by wading but it was too violent and deep. Once I had nearly got across when I had to wade back. Finally I found a bridge and watched it for some time before I went over because I thought the Germans would guard every bridge near Åndalsnes.

On the far side I soon came to the snow region, and could no longer avoid setting footprints. In the early Spring there had been an enormously heavy snowfall in western Norway, and even now, on 20th June, 1944 the snow still covered everything in the mountains. In spite of the deep snow, however, the birch trees up here were green, and I saw a cuckoo sitting in one of them with snow all around as far as I could see.

When I left the forest behind, only the barren mountains were before me, covered with snow. Soon the surroundings disappeared in the mist and I could only see a few hundred yards ahead. After a while I found myself at the end of the valley. Steep mountain sides, vast precipices rose before me. I could not get any further and felt trapped.

To the right of me, however, there seemed to be a possible way of getting up, there seemed to be a kind of valley behind the mountain edge near me. Maybe that valley led towards Eikesdal. I got up there. It was a narrow mountain edge. I had the feeling of balancing on top of a huge wall, a steep slope where I came from, and an enormous precipice in front of me. I looked down the precipice. There, two or three thousand feet below me was a green valley with a broad silvery river, a narrow road and a railroad. No doubt as to which valley I was looking upon. This was the Romsdal, the valley I wanted to avoid. The edge I had mounted was leading to the famous Romsdalshorn peak and the valley I had left was the Venge Valley. No possibility of getting to Eikesdal this way. I had to go back.

If the Germans found my footprints, they might of course follow them up the valley. I could not avoid that but I could avoid them finding my tracks leading down the valley until they had been to the end of it. By going back still higher up the mountain slope. This slope was the side of the Vengetind peaks, some of the highest and prettiest of the Romsdal Mountains. I walked in the mist in these slopes for most of the day. Mrs. Voile's sandwiches made a nice meal in the middle of the day later on I ate small pieces of the German bread.

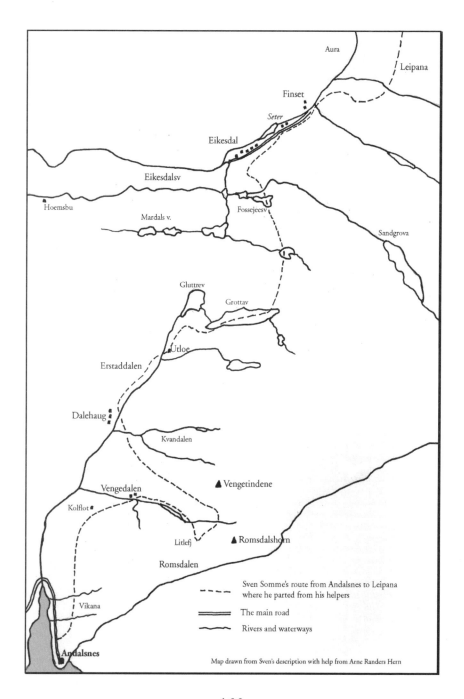

Aura

Leipana

Finset

Seter

Eikesdal

Eikesdalsv

Hoemsbu

Mardals v.

Fossejeesv

Sandgrova

Gluttrev

Grottav

Utloe

Erstaddalen

Dalehaug

Kvandalen

▲ Vengetindene

Vengedalen

Kolflot

Litlefj

▲ Romsdalshorn

Romsdalen

Vikana

Andalsnes

Sven Somme's route from Andalsnes to Leipana
where he parted from his helpers

The main road

Rivers and waterways

Map drawn from Sven's description with help from Arne Randers Hern

166

In the afternoon I came to another valley and went down through the birch wood which was wet from the fog. Whenever I touched a trunk or a branch I got a shower of water over me and was soon thoroughly soaked. At the bottom of the valley I waded across the river and soon reached a third valley. This one, I thought, would certainly lead towards the Eikesdal district.

There seemed to be a narrow road on the far side of the valley.

Two bridges crossing the river seemed to lead to this road. Were they guarded by the Germans?

I found a fir-clad hill where I could overlook both bridges and sat down to watch them. It was 5.00pm. On the side of the upper bridge two men were cutting wood with a hand-saw. There were some farms along that side of the river and I could see people moving between the houses. Everything looked normal and peaceful. I wouldn't take a risk however, and so I sat there, wet and freezing, watching the two men cutting wood, for two-and-a-half hours. At seven some women arrived at the upper bridge carrying milk pails. They went into a cow-shed and after a while came out with the full milk pails and went back to their farms. I went across the bridge. The men cutting wood saw me crossing so I could not avoid speaking to them.

"Good evening, that looks like heavy work you've got there."

"Not too bad. We get used to it. Where do you come from?"

We spoke about wind and weather and other indifferent things for a while and I told them I lived at Åndalsnes and was out for a walk.

I tried to make the conversation as natural and indifferent as possible. After a while they told me that no Germans had been here today and that there were very few Norwegian Nazis in this community. When I felt sure that these two men were not Nazis I said: "I have escaped from German captivity today and am trying to get across the mountains. Where does this valley lead?"

"You can't get across the mountains alone. There is a precipice at the end of this valley. Only local people know how to get up there. Across the mountains is the Eikesdal Valley but it is a long way to go-"

"I must try to get across. Can you let me have some food?"

They told me they were living further down the valley. They had no food here but I might get some food at one of the nearest farms.

"Do you know the people there? Are they reliable?"
"We suppose so."

"But are you quite sure? I would rather go ahead without further food than run into Nazis."

"We don't know them very well."

The men told me how to get over the precipice, but I had reservations about them because they became evasive and looked very suspicious. I took the precaution of asking the way to the Langfjorden and said I might just as well try that way.

Later on I learned the reason why these men appeared suspicious and reserved. It was because the Germans in Åndalsnes had recently sent out false refugees and had punished everyone who had given them food and shelter.

The farm near the bridge was the uppermost in the valley, there were some *seters* further up. I was tired, wet and cold, having walked for 16 hours since my escape and only rested two-and-a-half. Just now I was not very keen on climbing dangerous precipices and felt I had to get some rest before I could start anew.

I soon came to some *seters*. The houses were small like most *seter* houses in this part of the country. Most people do not live in the *seters* during the summer. They milk the cows there during the evening, sleep in the *seter* at night, milk the cows again in the morning and carry the milk down to the farms. They work the farm during the day and go to the *seter* again in the afternoon.

One of the *seters* was open so I went inside. There was a berth I could use and I found two fishing rods made of hazel-bushes, a piece of string with a fish-hook tied to each, such as a small boy might use for angling in small brooks. I stole the string and the hooks because they might be useful.

Through the window of another *seter* I could see a berth filled with hay. It looked like heaven to me.

169

There was a big padlock on the door, so I could not get in that way, but I succeeded in removing the window frame, crept in and lifted the frame in place after me. Some people passed the *seter* just as I finished the job but I felt quite safe. From the outside the *seter* looked deserted and closed.

I buried myself in the hay on the bed but there was too little to give any warmth. I was still very wet and cold which made me unable to sleep. It felt nice to stretch and rest for a while. In a corner I found some small rugs which I wrapped around my neck for warmth and was able to doze for a couple of hours.

Every now and then I heard people passing by the road only a few yards away from the hut. What were they doing up here so late at night?

Finally, when everything was quiet and I was freezing too much to lie quiet any longer I opened the window, crept out and put the window back in place. I started off at full speed for the precipice in front of me. It was nearly midnight, 22 hours since my escape and I had seen no Germans yet. They would not get me!

The night was cool and the air was crisp. The two hour's rest had done me good and I felt strong again. The road disappeared and there was only a narrow path left.

Suddenly there was a rush in the bushes near the path. A girl came towards me. It was too late to hide. She ran up to me seized my hand and said: "Don't be afraid, we have come to help you. We thought you would be less frightened to meet an ordinary Norwegian girl. My brother and a friend are up at the precipice looking for you. They'll soon be here. There is a barn across the river where we will hide you. We have brought dry stockings and food for you. Come along to the barn"

Again I surrendered unconditionally.

Chapter 14

ACROSS THE MOUNTAINS

The bridge was well hidden, the path to it was hardly visible. Trees were hanging across the river from both sides. Actually it was not a bridge only a single slender stock of birch-wood and an iron string to support the crossing.

Ragna went across in front of me. She went so steadily and fast it looked as if it was the easiest thing in the world. She was slender and fair with blue eyes, just as a Norwegian girl should be. She told me she was twenty-four.
.

We met her brother, André and his friend on the other side. André was a handsome boy of 19, his friend was a couple of years older.

Andre looked at my shoes. They were thin and worn and at present soaked from snow and wading.

"You cannot cross the mountains in these shoes. Try my boots to see if they fit."

He had a pair of brand new, solid boots, just my size, and we changed on the spot.

The barn was there and we crept inside, all of us. My new friends were eager to show me everything. The barn was half-full of dry hay from the previous summer and in addition to that they had brought bed-clothes and a pillow. When I buried in the hay I would be as snug as in an eiderdown.

They had a pair of thick dry stockings and a jersey too. I had to change at once. They had brought bread, milk, wafers and cakes, pork and dried mutton.

The two men I had spoken to at the bridge had told them they had met me. They did not believe I really was a refugee until they arrived home and heard about my escape and all the fuss the Germans had made at Åndalsnes. Ragna and the boys had been searching for me in the valley for quite a long time. The boys had been to the precipice and seen that I could not have passed there as there were no footprints in the snow up there. The eldest boy gave me a small book. It was from his sister with good wishes. It was the New Testament.

Ragna asked me if I could speak English. I said yes, I had even been a teacher in English.

"Then you must give me lessons. I have joined a course by correspondence and it is very difficult to know how to pronounce the words. How do you pronounce 'house', 'father', 'mother', 'brother'?" I promised to give her lessons.

They explained to me that I could not get up the precipice alone. They would get an experienced mountaineer to take me up there but I would have to wait until Saturday because it would look suspicious if they left their work and went to the mountains on a week-day. Meanwhile I would be quite safe here. The Germans had searched every house in Åndalsnes for me last night, and almost every house in the Isfjorden. They had sent soldiers out in every direction and several bloodhounds. The Oslo Express had been detained for eight hours. All the passengers had been lined up in a ware-house, face to the wall. Their luggage and even their pockets had been examined. I wonder if they thought I could have hidden there! My guard, a waitress and a mate on the *Hankø* had been taken to Dombås. The Germans had not been in this valley, and if they came here, they would probably not find the bridge and the barn. It would though, be safest, if I went to the precipice tomorrow morning. I would have a good view of the valley from there and could watch everybody coming up the road.

My new friends would bring me food every night and some magazines and books for entertainment.

I warned them not to let anyone know they were helping me, not even their closest friends. If they were caught they would be severely punished, may even be tortured or killed. Too many knew it already. They promised to keep the secret.

My valley, the Erstaddalen, was a beautiful spot. Huge blue mountains rose on three sides. Blinking snow-fields crowned their heads, hundreds of small waterfalls draped their sides and precipices. The bottom of the valley was covered with a dense forest of alder, birches and hazels. The bottom was soft green grass with an abundance of lilies-of-the-valley and other flowers.

I spent the days wandering about in this paradise, watching the birds and the foaming rivers. My barn was like a fortress with a river on either side. The water came from the snowfields and was cool and clear like crystal.

My friends came every night and brought me food and books. Ragna brought her English text book and had her lessons. She brought new friends too. One was Hans, aged about thirty, tall, meagre and full of fun. None of us had tobacco, but Hans brought me green dried stems of home-grown tobacco plants, a knife and brown paper. We carved the stem and prepared cigarettes from the carving and brown paper. The taste was awful but the effect was wonderful.

Sometimes we made a tiny fire and prepared surrogate coffee and my barn was at night a gay and pleasant centre. Ragna also brought me a shaving set, paper and pencil. I wrote a letter to Kristian Opstad. It said, 'I want a new name, Identity Card, a passport for the Eastern Boundary zone, money, ration-book, tobacco. Address: Jørgen, brother of Hjalmar. Expect to arrive there about 5th July.'

André went for a bicycle ride to the Langfjorden, where he met the local steamer 'Rauma' and gave the letter to the Captain. He handed it over to Kristian.

Saturday was the day of departure. I had been there since Monday night. Ragna arrived in the afternoon, bringing her text book and a parcel containing a hammer, some studs for strengthening my boot soles, boot grease, and a brush for the grease. She had thought of everything, even an iron-last but regretted it would have been too heavy to carry.

She had her English lesson while I was preparing my boots for the journey. Then she said there was a girlfriend of hers who wanted to give me a good meal before I left. She was in a *seter* half-a-mile down the valley. Ragna went a hundred yards in front of me down to the *seter*. If she waved her arms that would mean danger and I would have to hide in the forest. Signe was a pretty and very shy young girl. She shook my hand but hardly spoke a word while I was there. She had prepared a solid dinner consisting of pork cutlets, potatoes, jam tart and cream. The girls watched me eating. Afterwards all three of us had cakes and surrogate coffee together.

When I left, Signe shook my hand and said "Good luck." She said it so simply and sincerely. When she withdrew her hand there were 40 kroner left in mine. I feel sure that was all her property. How can one ever repay such a debt?

Later in the evening a man arrived at my barn. He was not very tall but broad shouldered and very well built. His face was sunburnt and weather-beaten, open and handsome. His eyes were clear and blue. He carried two pairs of skis and two rucksacks. I understood one of each set was for me.

I knew who this man was although he did not tell me his name. It may be well known to many British mountaineers who have been to Norway: Arne Randers Heen. He knew my name too.

He opened the conversation: "You would not have been arrested without reason and the Germans would not have made such a fuss about your escape unless you were a valuable prisoner. For years I have tried to be a member of an underground movement. I could do useful work because I know many Germans and all the German camps and fortifications in the Romsdal district. I have been unable to find an organisation to join and I hope that you can help me. Look here."

He unfolded a set of drawings and photographs. I recognised them. They were plans of all German fortifications in the whole of the county.

"I assisted an Estonian engineer in stealing these from a German safe. I took them to a person whom I believed to be a member of the Norwegian Secret Service. He did not believe they were genuine. When he had had them examined and they proved to be genuine he mistrusted me because I knew so much about the German establishments. Later on, he mistrusted me because I had hidden a Polish refugee and was court-martialled by the Germans and set free. Can't you see that I would be able to do useful work if only they would trust me? When you arrive in Stockholm go to General Ericksen and tell him I have fulfilled the task he set me, then put me in touch with your organisation."

We talked matters over and I promised to put Arne in contact with my organisation as soon as I arrived in Stockholm. Arne then went to sleep for a couple of hours in the hay.

A tall man crossed the river and approached the barn accompanied by two young men. I knew them all. They were Hans, André and Karl. Hans and André carried rucksacks, skis and some heavy constructions of wood. They intended to go with me across the mountains to Eikesdalen. Karl only came to say goodbye to me, he only carried a tiny paper bag, which he presented to me. It contained some green leaves of home-grown tobacco and a packet of cigarette papers. How I appreciated that gift! Tobacco was very scarce. I knew that there was no real tobacco at all in the valley. Hans was carrying green dried stems of home-grown tobacco plants and used to roll his own foul-smelling cigarettes from that sawdust - like stuff and newspaper. He had also offered them to me but I found both the taste and smell so dubious that I would rather do without.

The wooden constructions which Hans and Andre carried were window frames and a door for a stone hut that Arne and Hans had built in the mountains. Every little bit of equipment for the hut had to be carried on their backs from the valley 2,000 feet up the precipice and over the mountains. In order not to raise any suspicion amongst people in the valley over the reason for this trip, they had brought the framework along with them, telling people they intended to visit their hut in the mountains. People were used to seeing these keen mountaineers starting for week-end trips like this one.

After a mighty meal in the barn we said goodbye to Karl and at four o'clock in the morning made for the precipice. Hans and Arne were famed mountaineers and it was a great consolation to me that Andre was just as skilled in the art as I was.

All of us carried rucksacks, skis and sticks. The wooden frames were troublesome to carry so when we had walked for some minutes we split them into pieces by means of a stone and carried some parts each.

What a lovely morning! The rising sun gilded the snow-clad peaks and the glaciers above us. The valley was still in shadow but a chorus of bird-song rose against the sky. There seemed to be a robin or a song-thrush in every bush or tree. The birches and alders were dressed in their fairest green and the first lilies-of-the-valley were peeping out among the rich green grass. From the scree below the precipice we could see all the small *seter* huts and farms in the valley and below them a light cloud of mist was drifting slowly downwards over the river.

We followed a path through the wood and across the scree further up. The upper pan was covered with old hard snow and we proceeded slowly across it, kicking steps with our boots, then we started climbing the precipice. No path could be seen any more, but from olden times people had found their way up here to the vast mountain ranges above, shooting reindeer there and carrying meat and skins down the precipice to their farms in the valley below. It is impossible to pass there during the winter and furious avalanches run incessantly during the spring, making it impossible for trees to grow in the small patches of soil that can be found on the ledges on the mountainside, nor can any visible path be formed by the few feet yearly passing here.

So we started climbing. Far below us to the left we had the river throwing itself into a mighty waterfall from the top of the precipice, then jumping and spraying in the rocks in the bottom of the ravine, then finally floating quietly past the *seters* and farms far down in the valley. Up to the right we had an insurmountable precipice, so we slowly made our way towards the top of the waterfall. I did not like that ascent very much.

I crept and crawled up ridges and past ledges on the mountainside skis in one hand, sticks in the other, rucksack on back. Hans and Arne did not climb at all. They just walked upright, unworried, giving André and myself a hand when it seemed necessary. We had to cross several small glaciers which were hanging on the mountainside, I did it with the feeling that any moment I might rush 1,200 feet to the bottom of the ravine and it gave me some consolation to see that Andre felt the same. Over and up we came at last and standing at the edge of the precipice we caught a last view of the beautiful Erstad valley. I sent warm thoughts of gratitude to Ragna, Signe, Karl and all my other friends in the valley who had, at great danger to themselves, saved my life and given me all the support they were able. I promised that I would pay them a visit next summer when the war would be over. Would it be over? D-day was three weeks ago and the Allies had got a solid bridgehead in Normandy.

I did not feel as if I were fleeing. We felt sure that no German would dare, or even think of coming this way, so we considered ourselves quite safe. We enjoyed our journey as a trip. We sang and joked, we felt strong, free and happy, full of joy from the beautiful view we had from the edge of the precipice and it did not worry us much that we had a long, strenuous day before us. The mountains were ours. No German soldier had ever set his foot up here, nor was he likely ever to do so.

This was a new world, starting 3,000 feet above sea level. Here were valleys, hills and mountains, lakes and rivers, all covered with deep, compact snow. No path, no road, crossed this frozen landscape. No footprints of man to be seen. The mountains were high, but not so wild as seen from the Erstad Valley. Nor were the valleys so narrow and deep up here. Those below looked from here like deep and narrow cuts made with an enormous knife. How small and insignificant the houses, meadows and pastures, the roads and all the activity of man in the depths of the valleys, looked from here. From below he cannot even see this wild free world up here.

We put on our skis after a short rest and started crossing the mountains. Our first aim was a small hut at the border of a big lake, Arne and Hans knew the way and found the place but the hut was buried in deep snow. Not even the chimney was to be seen. The lake itself was nearly five miles long completely covered with ice. On this day, 25th June, there was only a small open space near the outlet.

We shouted, sang and called to each other as we went along: "It this the way to Stockholm?"

"Right O, just turn to the left at the second traffic lights." The sun was burning. All of us got very sunburnt that day. We halted for lunch on a nice slope. This was the highest point of our route, 4,000 feet above sea level. The heavy framework was unloaded here. The stone hut was only half-a-mile away. Arne found this to be a suitable opportunity of taking two or three photographs as a reminder of this most memorable trip.

Further on we crossed the tracks of reindeer and of an elk ox, and near the lake we also found tracks of another. Soon the hills started sloping down towards the Eikesdal Valley.

The sides of the Eikesdal are so steep that in fact they can only be descended at a very few spots. I realised now that it would have been madness for me to try to cross the mountains alone and without skis. First the Erstad precipice, then 25 miles across an unfamiliar mountain landscape and then how would I have been able to find my way down to the Eikesdal? Most likely I would have perished if I had ever succeeded in reaching the mountains.

I will not easily forget our descent. My three friends left their skis on top and all of us proceeded on foot. Arne and Hans were leading the way with Andre and myself following. We soon met with the first bushes and the slope got rapidly steeper. Halfway down it descended into a ravine. Andre and I crept slowly downwards clinging to the bushes when suddenly I heard a cheerful exclamation from Arne: "Here is the glacier!"

Yes, there was a steep glacier hanging on to the mountainside and ending in heaps of wild rocks below. Those two, Ame and Hans, threw themselves over the edge, sliding down on their boots at tremendous speed. To me they looked like spiders dropping down vertically leaving a thread behind. Andre and I watched them, hearts in our mouths, expecting to see them smashed against the rocks below, but a few yards from the rocks they made a sharp turn. This broke their speed and they then jumped from one rock to another as if it were nothing.

André and I kept to the bushes and gingerly made our way down, when eventually we passed the glacier and rocks we found the two of them lying asleep side by side on a soft layer of heather!

We could see the lower part of Eikesdal and most of the Eikesdal Lake from here. Right below us were the light green meadows of the Reitan Village and the farms bordering them peacefully. What a striking contrast between this wild ravine and the wide, flat meadows below. Then, beyond the farms, was the river, the well know Eira salmon river, running like a silver band through dark green pine woods towards the lake to the left. By the side of the river rising steeply like a wall, the eastern valley side, a precipice 3,000 feet high with hazel bushes covering the foot of it.

To the left was the lake, a long narrow fjord, both sides flanked by wild mountain scenery, and what colours! The mountains grey and blue with greenish-white glaciers like collars around their necks, mighty waterfalls spraying their dark sides. The lake itself was in shadow its waters greenish-black but with borders of deep jade green in the shallow parts.

> *Pretty is the country,*
> *I never saw it prettier.*

Thus sang Gunnar of Lidarende when he left his Icelandic farm 1,000 years ago.

On the narrow road winding between farms we could see the villagers walking peacefully between the meadows, meeting and speaking with each other, probably discussing how well their crops would harvest this year. There seemed to have been a good start so far. Some of the villagers had apparently discovered us and we saw them point in our direction.

We were not too happy about this as our trip should be

secret and now unfortunately we had been observed. We planned to keep to the hazel wood and if we met anybody I would have to keep silent, my dialect being different from the others. I was christened Karl Leirvik. If someone spoke directly to me I would say yes or no but not a syllable more.

We met two people in the forest. They had seen us coming down from the ravine and wondered where we had come from and where we intended going. We told them we came from the Isfjord and were making a Sunday trip to this valley and we intended to go back by the same route tomorrow morning. We had a chat with the two farmers and I kept in the background, uttering yes and no when I was spoken to directly. We then parted from them and made our way up the valley by the road those six miles to Finset.

I had been at Finset 24 years earlier with my father. It is a farm and travellers' station. How well I remembered Kristian Finset, the farmer. He was six feet tall, with broad strong shoulders and a mighty chest, well known over these parts of the country as a clever mountaineer and a helpful keeper of the tourist station.

Now his son Nikolai had taken over, I did not recognise him. I was introduced by Arne as Mr. Karl Leirvik. He said I had had a quarrel with the Germans about my duties in the National Labour Service and wanted to keep away for some time. Nikolai just said we could trust him. My friends ought to get up at three in the morning so as not to be observed by anyone else in the valley. As people would now know we had been here he would tell them that we had all gone back to the Isfjorden during the night.

My friends called me to say goodbye at half-past-three in the morning. I was awfully tired and did not envy them their strenuous walk across the mountains. I shuddered at the thought of the precipice they had to climb down to the Erstad Valley and wished them with all of my heart a 'happy landing'.

Chapter 15

MORE MOUNTAINS

Next morning Nikolai came into my room and sat down. I had the feeling that he wanted more than just a chat. He looked into my eyes and said without twinkling: "I am sorry I have forgotten your name, what did you say it was?"

I decided to tell him the truth. "I want you to know that it is dangerous for you to keep me here and hide me. As a matter of fact I was here twenty-four years ago."

"Are you Mr. Sven Sømme?"

I felt rather knocked out.

"Yes, I am. How did you know? Did you recognise me after all these years, or have you heard about me?"

"Well I thought I should recognise you, but I wasn't quite sure. I had calculated you would be around forty by now but you look younger."

"I am forty. But listen, I have fled from German captivity. I was going to be court-martialled as a spy and shot. A great many Germans are after me and if

186

they should find out that you have hidden me it will mean the gravest danger to you."

"Don't worry about that, but nobody must see you here. You must not leave this room, nor let my neighbours see you at the window. I'll go with you to the mountains very early tomorrow morning and show you where to go. Are you used to the mountains and outdoor life? Well then, write out a list of everything you need for the next ten days or so. Don't forget anything. You will not be allowed to leave my farm unless you are properly equipped for all events in the mountains. I will bring you tools and what else is necessary to repair your things for the journey. Don't be afraid of asking for things you may need."

I wrote a list comprising necessary food articles such as oats, bread, butter, pork, dried milk, etc., sufficient for about ten days. Nickolai brought me the things and he also brought me a rucksack. He offered me a rubber coat and a rifle as well, but I declined. The coat was too heavy and the rifle a too visible weapon. My principle was to carry just enough to survive and as light a burden as possible so as to be able to cover a great distance at a minimum amount of time. Finally, my luggage weighed about 20lbs including provisions.

When I had made everything ready Nikolai brought me a small parcel from his wife. It contained a towel, a piece of soap, thread, darning-yarn, buttons and some needles. How I blessed Mrs. Finset for these useful things later on!

Nikolai was sorry he had no map to give me. He had a map of telephone stations in Southern Norway scale 1:1 million, showing the main river systems and another map in 1:100,000 showing a small part of my way. On a piece of sandwich paper I made a rough sketch of the first 150 miles of my route and put it into my pocket.

We started at half-past-four in the morning, following a tourist path leading steeply to the mountains. Half way up we rested and Nikolai found three heavy planks which we carried on our shoulders further on. A friend of Nikolai, Edvard, a tall, strong man with blue eyes, fair hair and a good looking face met us there and carried one of the planks. They did not say what the planks were for and I did not ask.

It took us an hour-and-a-half to ascend the steep side of the valley, and the barren mountains lay before us, partly snow-clad. Nikolai thought skis would be of little use to me so we had left them behind. Soon we came to a deep and narrow canyon at the bottom of which a turbulent river hastened towards the valley below. Now I would see what the planks were for, they were just long enough to make a bridge across the canyon. Edvard tied a rope around his waist and tried the bridge, then it was my turn and finally came Nikolai.

We parted on the other side of the canyon. Neither of us spoke many words. Nikolai seized my hands, looked into my eyes and said: "Good luck to you! Take care of yourself and don't take any chances. Remember it is all up for you if they get you. And when you arrive in Sweden, please send me word so I know you are safe."

He said it so sincerely, so warmly, that I felt I had

never had a better friend than this gentleman of the valley whom I had known only for 30 hours.

Mrs. Finset told me later on that she had never known her husband more happy than when, two months later, he got my letter from Stockholm.

Nikolai and Edvard crossed the bridge again, took the planks away and were out of sight. Literally, the bridge was cut behind me, there was no retreat. My way was clear, onwards to Sweden.

The weather was fine, light clouds covered the sky, the sun breaking through now and then. A cold northern breeze made walking comfortable. There had been immense amounts of snow last winter. It still covered most of the ground here and in some places I had to climb old avalanches where the depth of snow might be 20 or 30 feet. The snow was melting rapidly now and hundreds of small streams and rivers were coming down from the sides, singing their gay song of spring. They were not always easy to cross. I had to wade across some of them, others were too deep, wide and rapid to wade across, so I had to walk upstream until I found a bridge of snow. There were many of these bridges but I wasted much time in finding them.

My way led through a wide and open valley and past long lakes which were now open. In sheltered places I could pass through small woods of birch trees. In other places dense fields of willow bushes gave me some trouble in crossing.

These lakes once formed part of a great hydro-electric scheme. Dams were to be built and the lakes turned

189

into reservoirs. The river flowing through them was to be transferred to another drainage system where big power stations would be built. The work was started during the First World War, when money was abundant in Norway and millionaires shot up like mushrooms. Barracks were built at the lakes and a new road was laid. Then came the post-war inflation and the work was abandoned.

After the invasion in 1940, the Germans were interested in building power works and factories in Norway. So they took up the old scheme and set some 2,000 men to work. Most of this work was conducted in the Sundal valley further north but the barracks at these lakes were partly restored and sometimes visited by engineers and labourers.

I kept a lookout in case any of the barracks should be inhabited. Late in the afternoon I came across a barrack at the upper end of lake Aursjøen where there was smoke rising from the chimney and people running between the buildings. I had to steal back some hundred yards and make my way around through wet marshes well out of sight.

Most Norwegian mountain plains were rich pastures during the summer and from olden ages the farmers in the valleys take their cattle to the *seters* in the mountains. These *seters* are 'summer farms'. They look like miniature farms with small, low buildings. A lodging consisting of one or two small rooms, usually connected to a 'milk room", a cow stable and a small barn. Frequently *seters* from several farms are built together, forming a kind of *seter* village. These villages may consist of as many as 20 or 30 *seters* and 50 or more small buildings.

Nikolai had told me there was such a *seter* village in my way. He felt sure it was not yet inhabited, as it was too early in the year, so he suggested I should stay there overnight.

I found the Gåsbuseter all right, and as it seemed deserted I examined all the buildings until I found one which I could enter by the window. The room was clean with stone floor, a bed, a table, a stool or two and a fireplace. The bed was filled with an enormous heap of wood-wool.

I did not dare make a fire because I had seen one or two men near a hut half-a-mile away, but I prepared a cold meal, then made myself comfortable in the wood-wool and fell asleep.

I heard the rain beating against the windows and dripping from the roof when I awoke. Through the window I could see the leaden clouds and fog drifting over the marshes. The turbulent river passing the *seter* village had grown during the night and I could hear it rushing by. The watershed between western and eastern Norway was only a few miles away and I had already left the snowfields behind me, only a very few heaps of snow being visible from my window.

I suddenly discovered that my garment was full of wood-wool and when I put my hand to my hair I found that it was full of wood wool as well. What a lovely sight I must have been and I could not help laughing heartily at myself.

It had ceased raining when I started walking again but the river near the *seter* had grown so much that I had to wade in knee-deep water on both sides of the bridge.

When I had covered a couple of miles I discovered I had forgotten the map sheet in the *seter*. As I had no difficulty in finding my way however I did not return to get it.

After a walk of about six miles I came to the next *seter* village. Nikolai had told me it was probably deserted so I made my way straight through it. Suddenly I stopped, just in front of me was a boy of about 18 cutting wood. His back was turned against me so he could not have seen me yet but if I ran away and he should happen to see me, what then? Would he not tell his people that he had seen a suspicious person in the mountains? Then it would be told from one man to another, possibly finally reaching the ear of an informer or a German. Therefore I decided to show a good conscience, went up to him and said, "Good morning!"

According to good old custom, he did not look surprised but answered my greeting quietly and friendly, asking where I came from and where I was going. I told him I was an assistant lawyer from Ålesund that I had been in Eikesdal on business, had some days leave and was taking this pleasure trip on my way back to Ålesund. At Dombås I was going to join my wife and we intended to cross the western Gudbransdal mountains back to Ålesund.

"It's a bit early in the year," I added to make my story more reliable, "but most likely these will be my only days off this summer, so I have taken a chance."

"Do you know," he suddenly said with a smile, "there is a road coming up the valley here from the south. When I was hiking up there two days ago, I was

Otteroy, where Sven was arrested in June 1944

(L-R) Henry Berg; Selma Moldsvor; Ingvall Moldsvor; Karl Weraas.

Ellie and Yuli reach Grasjoen, July 2004

Kristian Finset (above) with Yuli (left) and Ellie and (below centre) with his parents, Nikolai and Marit

Eikesdal, before descent

Looking back at Fokstugu
where Sven crossed under the railway line

Flag carried by Sven Sømme when he escaped from the Germans in June 1944.

The flag carried by Sven in 1944, and his shoes
returned by Selma after 60 years

Sven's signature (1947) in the visitors' book at Nesset

The Rondane mountains

The door carried by Sven into the mountains (see page 176)

Ellie (below, right) and Linda with Sven's account

Jo-Sevat Bjøntegård (above centre) with Ellie.
The house (below) where Sven met Jo-Sevat's father,
John, at Øvre Rendal in 1944

suddenly stopped by two German soldiers coming out of the wood. They had steel helmets and machine pistols and asked for my identity card."

"What in heavens name were they doing in this remote valley?"

"They were searching for somebody who had escaped at Åndalsnes."

"Oh," I said, "a Russian PoW?"

"No, no, he was a Norwegian."

"Who had made his escape at Åndalsnes? But how the devil could they expect to find the fellow up here?"

"Oh," he said, laughing, "you know how the Germans are."

I bade goodbye to the boy and continued my route. That road he had mentioned was the exact route I had taken. The Germans had been there two days ago searching for me and stayed overnight wherever they wanted without asking anyone, leaving the huts open behind them. And they might be there yet! Indeed, I felt I was a significant person. A week after my escape they were searching for me a hundred miles away in remote mountain valleys but they would not get me!

Apparently it would be dangerous to pass that valley by day and by the road. The nights were light too but a person would not be easily discovered in the twilight. I decided to go to sleep somewhere today and walk on by night.

I walked until I was well out of sight of the *seter* and found a suitable quarter for a sleep among some pine trees near the road but out of sight of it.

I had passed the watershed dividing east and west and now the Dovre Mountains were ahead of me, followed by the railway and the main road between Oslo and Trondheim, then the Rondane Mountains and finally I would arrive at my friends at Lake Atnasjoen. I fell asleep among the pines thinking again: 'They shall never get me!'

The first thing I saw when I awoke at about seven were two men on a hill about a thousand yards above me looking all over the landscape with field-glasses. I rolled aside into the bushes and kept watching the men. I could not see their garments clearly but when they turned round and walked some steps I could see the heels and soles of their boots reflecting the sun's rays. Iron heels, German boots? Most probably. They walked a few steps, then turned around again, using the field-glasses once more. When they were walking they kept in step which was very unlike Norwegians!

If they were Norwegians what were they doing up there with field-glasses at this time of year? There were no cattle or sheep in the mountains yet. The reindeer were protected at this time of year and if they were poachers they would not look for reindeer near the *seters*. The reindeer would be further up in the mountains. The most probable conclusion was that they were Germans searching for me.

As soon as they were out of sight I collected my things, had a meal and withdrew to a wood of birches further down. Ahead of me was a broad meadow belonging to a *seter*, a lake below it and the barren mountains above. I would have to cross that meadow and thought it best to wait for the twilight in the birch wood. I had about four hours to wait.

Suddenly I heard a rustling noise approaching in the brush and held my breath. A hare came jumping lazily through the undergrowth, collecting some grass here, some heather there, now and then stopping listening for danger. It passed me hardly ten yards away and then disappeared towards the meadow.

I reasoned that the Germans would make sufficient noise to frighten a hare a mile away so without further delay I made for the meadow and crossed it.

I did not go by the road down the valley but kept to the forest parallel to the road. Some miles down the valley the road crossed the river by a bridge and I made my way through the forest to the left saying goodbye to the road. I felt safe now.

I knew there was a big river to cross somewhere ahead of me and during my wanderings through the dense forest I kept thinking of how I would be able to cross it. Soon I heard the noise of rushing water. It was a swiftly flowing river fed by the melting snow in the mountains. Imagine my surprise when I found a solid bridge just where I met the river. There was a *seter* village on the other side which looked inhabited so I went a good way round in order not to awaken any dogs.

Now I had a steep mountainside ahead of me, then desert mountains for many miles, most of my way passing between 3,000 and 4,500 above sea-level.

Clouds had drawn over and it started raining just when I had passed the forest and had the mountains ahead of me. A cold northern wind was blowing up there and despite the steep hills I had ascended I felt cold. I was very happy indeed to have a set of good underwear in my rucksack, a present from Arne so I dressed with everything I had and kept marching on.

It was a dull morning, the peaks of the mountains were hidden in the clouds, the heather and bushes were dripping and I was soon wet to the skin. Fortunately my sandwich-paper map proved a good enough guide so I was never in doubt as to my route.

A broad open valley, the Grøndalen, was lying ahead of me. The landscape was flat and in the mist I could not see what was up and down or which way the river was running. My sandwich map could give me no information about this point, as it showed one continuous river across the watershed into two different valleys, one passing down the Foldal to the river Glomma, one passing down to the Gudbrandsdal. And now, where was the watershed? Later on I learnt that the map was correct but the river was wrong. It starts as a normal river on the southern slope of the Snøhetta Mountain, then after some miles divides into two branches one running west and the other east, a rather rare occurrence. To me it was an important question as I could only count on getting across near the watershed where it would be small. So I judged it to be to the right and made for it only to find a turbulent and broad river which was impossible to pass.

The only thing to do was to follow upstream towards

the watershed. I sat down on the river bank feeling a bit depressed. This would mean at least ten miles up and a similar distance down again. It was raining incessantly and the wind was blowing right through my clothes. Furthermore I was tired having walked all through the night and I would have liked to rest and have a nap rather than this purposeless walk up and down the river, but my blanket was too thin to keep me warm.

Never mind. My next important passage was ten miles away on the other side of the river, that was the crossing of the main road and the railway between Oslo and Trondheim. Six miles to the west of that crossing was Dombås with German Headquarters where by this time I would probably have been court-martialled and sentenced to death. Ten miles to the east of the crossing was another German station, Hjerkun, therefore if I could not pass that crossing by day without courting danger, I would cross it at midnight when, as now, it would be too cold to rest, so I may just as well spend the day in walking lazily. I had plenty of time.

A couple of miles up river there was a shallow ford which seemed possible to wade. The water coming down from the glacier of the highest Dovre Mountains, was extremely cold and after about a hundred yards of wading I could no longer feel my feet. When I had just ten or fifteen yards left of the river I came across a deep and turbulent channel which proved impossible to cross. I had to wade the whole distance back again to the northern bank. I made another attempt to cross further up which met with the same result so I had to resign myself to go on searching for the watershed.

When passing a marshy stretch I suddenly discovered some reindeer horns between the bushes, I counted six or seven pairs. My hunting instincts awoke, I imagined I was out stalking, gun in hand, trying to get as close as possible to the game without being discovered. So I went transversely until I had the wind coming straight down on me from the reindeer and proceeded carefully towards the herd. At about 150 yards one of them rose, it was a big buck with very good horns. Around the buck one deer rose after another, not six or seven, but dozens. I counted 25 but there were still some more. The buck ran away, perhaps 50 yards, then stopped, what a brilliant target he made! Then all the others started running and in a moment the whole herd was on rout at a tremendous speed through the marshes. Water and moss was spraying from their hooves making the rear-guard of the herd hardly visible through the spray. They ran towards the mountains forming a long row and in a few minutes were miles away in the mist.

I felt much more encouraged by this event and did not feel tired any more. My spirits rose and I felt again that I was free and happy. I had my troubles, who had not? But I had been prepared for conditions like these. My principle had been, just sufficient equipment to survive, and gosh, I would survive worse conditions than these. Two days walk and I would be among friends again.

About ten miles from where I first met with the river I found a bridge. There was a hut on the opposite bank where I tried in vain to break doors and windows open. A rest would have been welcome, why do people always lock their huts so securely? Why the devil do they? Don't they know that hundreds and thousands of good Norwegians in these troubled days are living as outlaws in the forests, in the mountains? Well, the doors and windows were bolted and as my only tool was a knife there was nothing doing, the only thing to do was to go ahead.

There were more huts in that mountain plain. I visited five of them that afternoon, inspecting the locks and bolts, trying to open them, cursing their owners. I lay down by the side of one of the huts, pulled my blanket over me and tried to sleep but it was too cold. I had to go on.

It was only nine in the evening when I was standing on the slope towards the railway. From here I could see both the road and the railway and the deep quiet stream between them in the bottom of the railway. I could see every house of the large *seter* village below me on this side, I could see the smoke rising from many chimneys.

At some distance I could also see the Fokstugu railway station and a busy locomotive working in the station yard. People were busy everywhere so I could not descend the slope for at least two or three hours.

I found a sheltered place among the hills, sat there freezing for a while, then I decided to prepare a very small fire. I collected some dry branches of juniper, broke them into five inch sticks and lit them, watching carefully that no smoke was formed, all the time placing myself between the fire and the valley below. It was a wonderful feeling to hold my hands close to the fire and feel the warmth penetrating my skin; what a blessed heat that radiated out from those tiny flames.

When my little fire had burnt down and all that was left was a small heap of glowing wood coals, I lay down on my back with the glowing coals under my bent up knees and spread my blanket over me to feel the warmth rising slowly everywhere under the cover, and I fell asleep almost at once, feeling extremely well and happy.

I awoke two hours later, trembling with frost, had a hasty meal and made for the village. There was no smoke from the chimneys of the *seter* village any more, nobody to be seen between the houses. The *seter* people go very early to bed and rise early in the morning.

I found a tunnel under the railway, prepared for a creek, and after having spied thoroughly in both directions, I crept through it and soon came to the bank of the river. It was swollen from the rain and the melting snow from the mountains, a dark, quiet and very deep river, running through the marshes.

It proved impossible to get across without swimming and I hated the thought of swimming in this ice cold water especially as I was already cold. I made my way back through the tunnel and soon found a bridge across the river further up. There was a narrow road leading from the bridge up to the main road which I followed. The main road seemed deserted as I walked along it for some hundred yards, when suddenly in the twilight I discovered shadows in front of me moving rapidly along the road. I halted, wondering what they could be, suddenly a shadow dashed out from the wood in front of me to the middle of the road and stopped there. Another shadow jumped up beside it and stopped likewise. Now I could see they were hares, sitting erect in the road, ears straight up. Then as if a shot had sounded they both ran away at a tremendous speed and disappeared beyond a turning in the road further ahead. Apparently this main road was the playground of the hares during the night, there was no traffic so they used it for their nightly competitions.

From the hills above the *seter* village I had seen a route into the mountains on the southern side of the crossing. The hills were high but not very steep and there seemed to be a valley leading into a mountain pass. My map was not very accurate but I guessed I would hit upon the upper part of the Grimsdal Valley if I crossed that mountain pass. It had long ago ceased raining and had cleared up. The northern wind had calmed down and it had become very cold. I had made it a habit to take a meal every two hours, then lie down and rest until I was cold, then go on again. This was quite practical as a short rest gave me sufficient strength to go on for a couple of hours and I felt that I could go on for days like this. I had only about 50 miles ahead of me through the mountains to Lake Atnasjøen, and perhaps I could make the whole distance in 24 hours.

The valley in the hills proved to be a disappointment, there was a ravine or canyon with a turbulent river at the bottom of it and the sides too steep to climb. I took a more easterly route which was flatter, with very short vegetation, well suited for walking without a path. There were many hares in the hills, they seemed to come from nowhere. Suddenly there was one, two or three hundred yards above me, it disappeared when I approached and then another one would appear in a different place.

It was three o'clock in the morning and the sun would soon rise over the mountains in the north-east. The grey nightly colour of the hills slowly gave way to more warm, blue and violet colours and suddenly one of the peaks to the right turned purple. The purple spread to the other peaks then crept slowly down towards me.

A deep ravine suddenly opened before me; there was a belt of old hard snow edging the nearest side of it. I had to climb down it, cross the ravine and ascend the opposite steep side.

The snow was frozen so my boots left no foot-prints. When it started sloping down I had difficulty in getting safe foot-holds. Luckily I had cut a thick stick in the forest below and it now became useful. As the glacier became steeper I had to thrust my stick into it and kick a foothold for every step. It was a long and troublesome process to get down but finally I reached the bottom of the valley and jumped over the creek. It was then I discovered that it was so cold that the spray from the creek had glaciated the stones with a thin cover of ice.

I had to cross three such ravines, one after the other, and when I finally reached the mountain pass, the sun had disappeared and all was covered with mist. I was now 5,000 feet above sea-level and the old hard snow covered everything with only odd stones protruding at intervals. I was lucky to find an ancient path leading through the pass. It was marked with small cairns, most of which could be seen above the snow, and I need never be in doubt as to my way.

In one such place where the snow was at least ten

feet deep a stream had cut its way through it and formed a canyon with vertical sides, just too broad to jump across. I lost an hour searching for a passage, eventually found one, and continued along the path. Soon I was on bare ground again when I heard a familiar sound, the cries of a lapwing. Only a few years before the lapwing was only distributed along the south and west coast of Norway but after 1930 it had spread to the eastern counties and to some alpine marshes. I had not expected to find them in the Rondane Mountains, five thousand feet above sea-level. Here they were, the male sitting proudly on a stone, the female running between the boulders.

The mist had dispersed and the sun came out. A cold, cold breeze had sprung up but I managed to keep fairly warm walking. On a big flat stone near the path I laid down for a nap and when I awoke I saw two men against the sky along the back of a peak only a few hundred yards away. One of them carried an enormous rucksack, perhaps both, I could not see clearly.

They were certainly not Germans, probably not tourists, but who were they? I came to the conclusion later that they were commandos or partisans who were probably living in the mountains.

Whoever they were, I did not want to be observed and I was glad when, after some minutes, they disappeared.

The mountain plain seemed endless, I kept on marching hour after hour along the cairns. My thoughts worried me as I was thinking of my family, my wife, my old mother and of my friends and I discovered that my heart was being turned into stone. Did I love anyone any more? Could I love any more? I was passing mountains famed for their beauty and I was indifferent to them. The lapwings I had seen did not raise any feeling of delight, of joy, as they would have done under normal circumstances. I just coldly noted the fact that I had observed the species far away from their usual area of distribution. It was a zoological fact and I was a zoologist.

I thought of the Germans and found I could feel no enmity towards them. The memory of my narrow escape did not raise any feeling of excitement. Even thinking of the sentence of death that awaited me at Dombås caused me no horror. My heart was numb.

Was it from exhaustion? No, I did not feel very tired. Had I gone through too much? No, I did not think that I had. Was I getting old? The thought seemed ridiculous, I still felt young.

I could remember now, I felt somewhat like this the previous winter when I was conducting my illegal work at night in my lodging at Midsund. I performed tasks automatically, stubbornly, but without emotion. I did the work because I was intellectually convinced that it was right, but I did not feel good and my heart was dead within me. Beyond my thoughts was the feeling that I was alive and that I was a Norwegian and that I loved my country. My country needed me to do illegal work so I did it.

I found no satisfactory explanation for this condition. Was I alone in feeling it? Did the partisans feel the same? Or the parachutists who had been dropped from Allied planes and were living in the forests and the vast mountain plains all over the country? Would that feeling last after I had returned to normal life? I felt it might and this troubled me.

The mountain plain was sloping gently towards the south-east. Small streams were hastening downwards. In the afternoon I got among the birch woods, the ground clad with heather, grass and juniper, with here and there some open meadows and *seter* houses. A sort of road wound along and a broad shallow river running to the south-east. The massive Rondane Peaks rose to the south and west of it. Some of them exceeding 6,000 feet. There was no doubt this was the Grimsdal Valley, I had arrived at where I was hoping to be.

Right below me was a couple of large buildings, busy women were running between the houses. This must be the Grimsdalen tourist hut and to the right of it was a large *seter* village with numerous small pastures between low stone walls. Cows and goats were grazing everywhere. There were horses wandering about freely on the plain near the river. The whole valley presented such a picture of peace and friendliness I found it difficult to accept that I was an outlaw who did not harmonise with this scene. I had to be careful and must not be observed.

I flung myself down between the rocks. The ground was covered with a dense coat of short heather, soft like a mattress. Whitish-violet alp anemones *(anemone vernalis)* were peeping up through the heather everywhere. I have never seen so many of them in one place and I felt the temptation to pick a large bunch of them but what use would that be now?

Mountain anemones, my favourite flower. They belong to the mountains where in early spring the first snowless patches appear, they peep up from the ground, pudgy buds, clad in a fur coat of grey, silken hair. When put in a small vase the crisp, clean, wax like flowers will come out in a few days. Towards the night it will close again and the fur clad sepals will shelter it against the frost. They are flowers of freedom. The Germans seldom dare to move so far into the mountains that they see the mountain anemone and even if they do they are apprehensive and anxious to get back to what they call civilization.

Perhaps I was not as careful as I ought to have been when I left my hiding place between the rocks and started down the slope near the *seter* village, but I was shivering with frost and only longing to continue my walk. Maybe they observed me from the *seters*, maybe not. I crossed the river and followed the narrow, winding road down the valley. The way seemed endless, I kept walking for hours without seeing anyone.

A few months later I was walking on the river plain of the Spey, a Scottish valley, that reminded me so much of the Grimsdalen. I cannot explain the conformity between these two valleys which in many respects are so extremely different. The Grimsdalen bordered by 6,000 ft. peaks with dark ravines and glittering glaciers, steep sides and birch trees bordering them. The Spey Valley with its rounded hills and distant mountains with pine forests at their feet. Perhaps there is some resemblance in the river plains, in their vegetation, or in the nature of the quiet rivers, both running over a bed of boulders and coarse gravel. I cannot explain it.

Late in the evening I had left the steep mountains behind me. The right river bank was steep and sandy, perhaps a hundred feet high, beyond it was a wide and open plain covered with heather, grass, reindeer moss and juniper, here and there broken by belts of low birch trees. I left the Grimsdalen there, climbed the bank and struck out across the open ground.

To the left of me I had the low round Østerdal hills, and to the right the mighty Rondane Mountains. After a few miles across the plains I would meet with another valley and another river, the Atna, also heading to the Rondane Mountains.

I dropped down on the soft carpet of reindeer moss and covered myself with my blanket. It was not so cold any more and I thought I might have an hour's rest to renew my energy. How tired I was! My body longed for a rest, how nice it felt to kick off those heavy boots and stretch my limbs on that soft reindeer moss.

I did not notice until then that the air was full of mosquitos; as soon as I stopped, these hungry devils came swarming from nowhere to satisfy themselves from my sweet blood. Nazis they were! Yes, they were Nazis, fed on propaganda and damned lies, sucking sweet and warm blood from honest patriots.

I pulled my blanket over my head. Holy Moses, I could see the whole landscape through it. Was it really so thin? The mosquitoes punctured the skin of my right hand right through it. Well I had gloves but those indecent beasts found all my weak points. My knees were almost bare, my trousers were worn thin. My ears touched the blanket and the mosquitoes found them. Damn it, I had better march on.

The sun set in the north west at eleven, Another nightfall that still found me marching. I knew the region very well, every turn of the road, every pool in the river. How often had I been fishing in this clear little Atna river? It was clear like crystal originating from the glaciers of the Rondane Mountains, running through a canyon in the slate rocks and finally coming through the pine forest into the open morainic plains of the upper Atna valley on a bed of boulders. The trout are silvery and cautious; they despise worm or a wet fly and will take only a dry fly. Only the previous summer I had one of my great dry fly day's here catching seven pounds of silvery Atna trout.

The Atna Valley is only 2,000 ft. above sea-level and there are quite a number of small farms in the river plain. None of them are very old, 200 years ago nobody was living here. The nearest farm was 40 miles further down, near the main valley of the River Glomma. These parts were only occasionally visited by people from the Gudbrandsdalen Valley who crossed the mountains hunting reindeer or fishing for the silvery trout or the purple char. Wolves were abundant in the mountains and still now and then cross the regions and the brown bear had its home in these forests. Then audacious colonists settled here, ploughed the brown soil and built their low timber houses, and now there is a farm for every mile of the valley. How well they fit in this lovely landscape, those low red-painted houses with white window frames and turf roofs. Every farm looks like a little village. There is the main building resting upon a white foundation wall, the barn and the cow stable, the washhouse, the sheep house, the implement house, the wood shed, the old folk's house, the bake house and four or five other small houses, all of them spread in the most pictorial confusion, not to forget the tall white flag-staff as a centre of the whole. All these tiny houses look clean and proper, the windows are full of flowers and framed with white lace curtains. The people who inhabit them look likewise tidy and they always seem to be content. I know all the farms by name and almost all the inhabitants.

The sun rose at three in the morning and found me still walking. I had followed the new main road for a couple of miles and then made my way through one of those farm villages up to the old road which is winding and turning up and down hill through the low pine forests of the valley side.

I knew the farmers here too, they were Nazis but I walked boldly straight through their farmyard, conscious that they were sleeping and that they kept no watch-dog. On top of the hill above the farm I flung myself down and slept for an hour. It was just here my wife and I came down from the mountains on skis last Easter, three or four months ago. We found foot prints of a capercaillie that had been circling round, playing in the forest, dragging its wings in the snow, and as we were studying these strange circles a beautiful red fox came towards us from below became aware of us and disappeared with long jumps into the thicket.

Now I heard the cock of a ptarmigan scolding among the trees not far away. 'Rack-gack-gack-garrr'. Its pronunciation is truly Scottish, a bit staccato with long rolling r's. As I stopped to listen a red fox came streaking from that direction, probably the same one that we had seen last Easter, but how poor he was looking! His colour was spot-wise red, spot-wise rusty, he was ragged, his fur was falling off in large patches and even his tail was uneven. He was moulting. He was unaware of me and jogged lazily along, now and then turning his head as if to see whether the ptarmigan cock was following. Then he sat down among the heather, yawned and licked his nose and lips. I spoke to him and told him what I thought about his garment; he just looked at me, yawned once more as if to say he did not care about my opinion, then rose and walked slowly up the hill and was soon out of sight.

At half-past-five I was outside the fence at Nesset, a small farm belonging to the Norwegian Academy of Science. My friends Hjalmar and his sister Inga were living there. They would probably get up at six, Hjalmar to look after his horse, Inga to milk the cows. There was a possibility that the Gestapo might know I had friends here. They may have found photographs and letters in my belongings at Midsund, and they might guess I would pass here. Therefore I did not go inside at once but sat down among the bushes outside the fence watching the door. I felt cold and tired and pulled my blanket over me, though through the blanket I could overlook everything. I could also see the beautiful blue Atnasjøen lake below the farm but I was much too tired to notice its beauty. I only noticed the damned mosquitoes had started to take an interest in my poor blood again and I heard them singing outside my blanket. Nevertheless I must have fallen asleep for a moment and when I awoke, I saw the door in front of me opening and Hjalmar came out. He stretched and yawned, then went to the stable. Everything was looking normal so I pulled myself together, knocked at the door and went inside.

Inga was just coming out of her bedroom. She is working much too hard, is always late to bed and correspondingly tired in the morning.

"Good morning Inga. I want some milk and a drink."

"I'll give you milk", she replied rather harshly, "but you'll have to keep yourself with spirits."

Then she stared at me, her mouth opening more and more, and suddenly she cried "Sven!" and flung both her arms around me.

Chapter 16

RESPITE

Inga did not usually receive me that way when I visited the farm but they had heard I had been arrested. They knew the matter would be serious for me and they had not heard of my escape. Inga's embrace was a spontaneous reaction of joy that I was free. When a few minutes later Hjalmar arrived, he smiled broadly and shook my hand so I feared my arm would break off. Ruth was also there, she was sleeping in another building and I called her and asked her to prepare my breakfast for me.

We had a council of war. Nobody must see me so I was put to bed in Ruth's bedroom and slept like the dead until four in the afternoon. They called me with a splendid dinner and plenty of hot water, Hjalmar gave me the necessities for shaving. How was I looking? My beard was a week old, I was dirty, fagged, sunburnt and lean from the mountain walk. My clothes were equally ragged and dirty. No wonder Inga did not recognise me at once, but I felt extremely well and fit and was surprised that my limbs were not stiff after the rest.

Hjalmar was busy that day, through the window I could see him running to and fro collecting things and bringing them together. At ten the people in the neighbouring farm went to rest and I was allowed to take part in the preparations. At eleven everything was ready, an enormous heap of luggage had been collected. Each of us took his or her part of it and all four of us went down the steep hills to the lake. We rowed across it to the western side, where, in six miles there was only one farm and that one belonged to Inga's and Hjalmar's parents. I could feel safe in these deserted parts.

There were several reasons why I did not proceed towards Sweden at once. First I learnt that there were many Germans along the route that I had intended to take. I would have to work out a new more southerly route which meant that I would have to pass two or three big rivers. Next, I would try to obtain indirect communication with my family in Oslo in order to warn them and to learn whether my wife had gone to Sweden.

We found a remote spot under a hill in the forest. On top of that hill I had shot two capercaillies six weeks before, it was a lovely place indeed. The ground was covered with juniper and heather and the hills around had a thick carpet of reindeer moss. Most of the trees were pines but with a few spruce in between, we chose a group of three or four spruce as the most suitable place for a tent. The ground was first covered with short branches of spruce and juniper then with a thick lambskin. Over that we erected an ordinary white tourist tent, then dressed it with a grey military tent.

We were sorry to see that from some distance it was much too visible but Hjalmar had brought an axe and went away to cut down some small spruce and birch trees nearby. We re-erected these small trees by means of wire around the tent so they looked like a natural thicket, then covered the tent with branches of spruce, and my lodging was ready. It could hardly be spotted at a distance of 30 yards. In fact, the first time I left it to go to the lake, I had a hard job finding it when I came back.

The inside presented the most comfortable lodging I have ever had in the field; heather yes, and boulders on the bottom, followed by spruce branches, then heavy lamb skin, a luxurious sleeping bag, and a pillow, then two tents, the camouflage of branches, the artificial thicket and the forest around it. Indeed the place was so sheltered that hardly a breath of wind could reach it. Yes, the mosquitoes soon discovered it and it became their favourite place. I wonder how many regiments and divisions of them I killed during the three-and-a-half weeks I lived there.

Hjalmar was very busy with his farming. He and his horse Satan were working from six in the morning to late at night. There were hundreds of large and small tasks to undertake. In addition to the work on the farm, he was expecting guests, mostly scientists, for their summer holidays, and was tidying and preparing everything to receive them.

On that first night in the tent he asked me: "Have you got any tobacco?"

I said no, and he shouldn't worry about it as I had been without tobacco most of my way across the mountains and it was not a necessity to me.

"What do you smoke? Pipe? Cigarettes? Have you got a pipe? Well then I will get you one."

He left the farm the following morning and was away for one day and one night. He was back in my tent on the second day.

"Here" he said, filling my lap with tobacco, cigarettes and a pipe.

"Smoke! I will bring you more when it is finished. There is always a need of tobacco when one is unemployed. You are my guest here and shall not suffer from any shortage. Just tell me what you want and I will bring it to you. I can easily get you anything you require. Have you got a shooter? Well, you will need one, I will get you one."

Inga and Ruth used to turn up late in the evening bringing food! Fried trout or char with pink flesh, bread, potatoes, milk, sweet and sour cream, cakes, sweets, meat - everything! I had a store of delicious food in a corner of the tent.

Hjalmar said: "Do they bring you enough food? Do you like cream? Do they bring you enough? I will tell Inga to bring you some more."

I turned day into night, it did not make much difference as sunrise followed three hours after sunset, and there was only a short period of twilight between them.

Ruth lent me a nine-and-a-half feet split cane trout-rod and towards night I went out fishing along the shore of the lake. There was not much to be caught, in fact there were hardly sufficient to provide trout for my breakfast. I used to return to my tent at five in the morning, light a small fire, watching carefully that no smoke rose from it, and cooked my breakfast. Then I slept until 1.00pm and had a solid lunch. At 3.00pm I arrived on 'my stone' which was a big piece of rock at the border of the lake. On sunny days I undressed there and lying absolutely naked read some English book that Ruth had brought me. Later on she started bringing me worn stockings too which I mended. I did it carefully because I had plenty of time and one pair a day was a suitable dose. When it was raining, as it sometimes was, I withdrew to a natural cave in a rock near by, reading or darning stockings there. I also wrote an up to date diary of all my adventures which I hid in the cave intending to retrieve it after the war. Ruth, who knew about it, took care of it shortly after my departure, because the mice had started taking an interest in it.

I had a daily time of conferences on 'my stone', between three and five in the afternoon. I received friends there, or more correctly a few of my intimate friends who were guests at the farm during their summer holidays. They were Professor Werenskold, his wife, and their daughter of one-and-a-half, who was my godchild. The eldest daughter of four was never allowed to see me because she could talk.

Through Mrs. Werenskold I could communicate with my relatives in Oslo. My wife had gone underground as soon as I made my escape and was to go to Sweden shortly. Everything was well and nobody had suffered because of me. It was a great relief to me to learn this. Ruth also communicated with my mother and got a message through to her and my wife that I was safe.

When my father was still alive he used to whistle a certain signal outside our cottage when he came home for lunch. We also used that signal as a call to each other for instance on camping tours, etc., and there was a reply to it. It was a stanza from one of the Wagner operas but after my father died in 1923 we ceased using it.

One day, as I was eating my lunch in my tent, I heard the family signal being whistled in the forest outside. I whistled the reply but found it difficult as I was deeply moved. The whistler could be none other than my brother Knud!

I rose to my knees and peeped out. Yes, there was a funny looking fellow wading through the heather towards my tent. It was raining and he wore a raincoat of some greenish-brown colour, a peculiar rain-hat, short oilskin tubes to protect his knees from getting wet and rubber boots. I could not help laughing even though, in fact, his appearance was a solemn event.

Knud was living in Halden, south-east of Oslo, close to the Swedish border. As soon as he heard of my escape he left his home and went to Oslo to avoid being taken as hostage. He had arranged with friends that a message should be sent to him if any foreigner was asking for him. His wife and two children were in the country and were instructed to go to Sweden by rowing boat if they received a certain message. It was only a short distance across the sea to Sweden.

As Knud would have to stay away for some time he took his fishing rod, his sleeping bag, and his bicycle, went by train to the Gudbrandsdalen Valley and by

217

bicycle across the mountains to Lake Atnasjøen. Knowing I had friends there he went to see Hjalmar in order to ask him whether I had passed this way on my route into Sweden.

"If you want to see your brother," said Hjalmar, "I can take you to him. I have got him in a tent two miles from here."

He took him across the lake in his boat.

There he was, my brother Knud, apparently just as glad to see me as I was to see him, both of us were moved, neither of us would show it.

"Knud," I said, in order to get rid of that lump in my throat, "I would advise you to become a refugee. It is a poor life you are living, you need ration books for everything and get lousy rations of ill tasting food. You spend lots of money and get very little back for it and as you are living in a town you have to queue for everything. Look at me, I have no money, no ration book, not even an identity card. Everyone is kind to me, I have never had such plentiful food as I get now. I have plenty of tobacco. They bring me everything I need and charge me nothing. I have never had better friends than I have now. Be a refugee and be happy. Look at my lodgings, when did you sleep in a sleeping bag on lambskin with a pillow under your head and a double tent over you?

"And such an abundance of mosquitoes" said Knud.

He had however 'Kikubotan' spirals in his rucksack. Which soon killed all the mosquitoes inside and became a relief during the days and nights to come.

Knud had had an 'underground' meeting with my wife Olaug. She was living alone in a flat belonging to some friends and was in contact with the 'export' organisation. Any moment she could be ordered to go to Sweden, and she was not allowed, even for a moment to leave the telephone. She had a trying time but was in good spirits.

They had discussed some peculiar problems, among them the question of who, if any of them, should go to prison as 'hostage' because of me. They agreed it had to be Olaug, firstly because the Germans might kill their victims at an eventual capitulation and would be less inclined to shoot women than men, secondly because Knud had a wife and two children to take care of and Olaug had no one but me, the cause of all the trouble.

Knud was not as yet suspected by the Gestapo so he was free to go where he wanted. Living in Zone East he also possessed a special certificate which permitted him to travel within the Eastern Zone bordering to Sweden. It was very difficult for other Norwegians to obtain permission to travel into these eastern regions. I was going to cross Zone East on my way into Sweden.

We now planned a new route for me. Everything was much simpler now I could send Knud in advance to arrange it. I wanted to contact some of my friends further east in order to arrange my crossing of the three big rivers, Glomma, Rena and the Klara. The bridges would probably be closely guarded so I would have to be taken across in boats. Knud had maps and we traced a route on the map. I asked Knud if he would go to an old friend of mine, Seming, who had a farm on the eastern bank of the river Glomma and see if he could help. Then he could go to another of my friends in the Rendal Valley near Rena and see what he could manage. Perhaps my friends there could even arrange my crossing of the third river, the Klara, as well.

I invited Knud to share in one of my luxurious meals after which he left me and went back to the farm. Hjalmar had put him in contact with a farmer ten miles up the valley and Knud cycled up there to establish himself as Mr. Jacobsen before he went to see Seming and the Rendal people. He visited me again before he left and I could not help worrying what would happen to him if the Gestapo were looking for him. Would he be arrested on his trip? Would his wife be taken in order to prevent his escape? There was little use in such speculations and off he went.

One or two days after his departure Hjalmar gave me a pistol; it was an enormous weapon, a Colt M.25 weighing at least a pound. The first time I put it in my pocket it went right through and I had to pick it up again from somewhere near my right knee. Inga provided me with a piece of cloth and I tailored a new, solid pocket in my trousers just fit for my new artillery.

I always carried it along with me in order to get used to it. I practised handling it quickly and 'shooting two Germans'. I knew that it was of the utmost importance, in case of an emergency, to be thoroughly familiar with the weight, balance and every detail of the pistol. I practiced getting it out of my pocket quickly, I took it to pieces every day, charged and uncharged it. I tried aiming but could not shoot, firstly because I had only nine cartridges, secondly because the noise would carry to the farms near the lake. One night, however, I fired two shots in order to see where I would hit the two Germans and found I would hit their bellies. Later on I learnt that my neighbours, Hjalmar's parents, heard the shots and wondered what was going on.

One day Jørgen turned up with a young student, Johann, whom I had never seen before. He brought me news from my organisation in Molde, he had been sent with messages from my colleagues there. He brought me everything I had asked for in my letter from the Isfjorden shortly after my escape at Åndalsnes, money, ration cards, and identity card, a passport for the 'Zone East' both with my photograph but with different names. Everything had been carefully sewn into his clothes and cap. There was also a letter written in invisible ink and the developer packed inside it! A nice touch indeed.

The letter said that there had been great joy everywhere in the Romsdal district because I had tricked the Germans, particularly among the young. 900 men and some hounds had been sent out in search of me. The informer Mathiesen had also left Molde dressed for mountaineering probably in order to 'help me' but he had returned after a short trip. Everything was well, no one had been arrested lately and the Germans had evidently given up searching for me.

Johann did not know what had happened to my belongings but he did know that at least my library had been saved. I was happy to learn that because I had valuable literature on freshwater biology that I had collected during nearly twenty years. I asked Johann to take greetings back and to tell my friends

221

that everything was well and that I felt confident that I would get safely in to Sweden.

I now had an identity card and passport but could I use them? Certainly not as they were both complete with my photograph, possibly the same one that the Gestapo had sent to all their departments during the hue and cry. If somebody on my way should ask for papers of identification, be it Norwegian or German police or soldiers, I would have no alternative but to shoot at once and this I decided to do.

"Your passport please."

Pang-pang.

That would be the way to do it.

When Ruth and Inga visited me one night one of them asked me if I sometimes had dismal dreams, for instance that I was punished by the Gestapo, going to be tortured or shot. I told them of the only dream I had had so far since my escape. I dreamt that Hjalmar and I were out to see the capercaillies playing in the forest. We were creeping through the heather when suddenly it struck Hjalmar that he should dress like a caper in order to try to get close to them. He crept into a heap of feathers and soon was several yards in front of me running through the heather like a caper. While he was away a caper hen passed me at a few yards. I whistled to Hjalmar, whispering to him that he should come back as there was a hen close to me. He came back asking me where she was and when he finally had sight of her, only a yard or two away, his eagerness was so great that he forgot he was a caper and thought he was a dog. He ran up to the hen sniffing her and wagging his tail of feathers eagerly. I awoke and found myself alone in the tent roaring with laughter. That was my only dream as long as I stayed at Lake Atnasjøen.

Hjalmar came to me one day and told me there was a band of partisans in the valley. Some paratroopers had been dropped in the mountains and were training young men from the valley as partisans. They were taught how to use modern small arms, Bren guns, sten guns, machine guns, hand grenades and so on, and also how to use explosives in sabotage, how to blow up bridges, railways and roads, etc. Hjalmar himself was an instructor in small arms and was organising small groups. His men were trained in shooting in the mountains. He used to bike through the valley with a machine gun on his bicycle on his way to the course and how he enjoyed it!

It would be easy for him to contact the paratroopers. During the next few nights they were expecting a plane from Britain to drop necessities. They were in daily radio contact with the Norwegian Headquarters in London and they could ask London whether the same plane that made the drop could pick me up and take me directly to Britain. If a sea plane were sent it could land on the lake.

I thought this was a good plan and asked him to contact the paratroopers and get them to ask London. To tell the truth every day that went by made me more nervous about my coming march to Sweden. I was unemployed and getting lazy which made the difficulties ahead seem to grow with every passing day and they started worrying me. Hjalmar's plan would solve all my difficulties.

There was nothing to prevent a British or Norwegain plane from landing on lake Atnasjøen and taking off again. I might get a rowing boat somewhere and leave it in the middle of the lake when I entered the plane. This would solve all problems.

Hjalmar returned a couple of nights later. He had met with the paratroopers, they had asked London and got this reply: 'A plane landing on the lake would be reported to the Germans. Their attention would be drawn to the district and it would not be wise. London would prefer to give me an escort of two well armed paratroopers in full uniform through Zone East to the border'.

I asked Hjalmar to convey my sincere thanks to the paratroopers and to tell them how much I appreciated their offer. I would, however, prefer to go alone in civilian clothes as I felt this to be less ostentatious. I felt ashamed, I had indeed behaved like a coward.

Sometimes Hjalmar and his brother Jørgen would come to me by night and suggest a small excursion. We might go trolling for big trout on the lake or angling for smaller trout in some of the clear mountain streams. Such excursions were very welcome to me and I will never forget those crisp and clear nights, the glorious sunsets and the wonderful sunrises. How can I ever forget Jørgen's face when he caught a five pound trout with trolling! He was a professional fisherman and he must have caught dozens of big trout in his life and this one was certainly not the biggest but I have never seen anybody more fully engaged in a fight than Jørgen when he caught that five-pounder, never watched any face more intently concentrated upon a struggle. Every movement of the fish was reflected in his eyes. I had far more pleasure from watching him than I would have had in playing the fish myself.

Another night when Hjalmar and I were using gill nets for trout we observed an animal trying to swim across the lake which just there was a thousand yards across. It was a squirrel and when we approached it swam towards us and tried to get on board but its sharp claws could not get a grip of the painted side of the boat so I tried to give it a hand. In no time it was on my shoulder and jumped to the gunwale then ran along the gunwale from stem to stern and back again. Once more it jumped to my shoulder then to the gunwale, then across Hjalmar from stem to stern, from stem to stern at an incredible speed again and again. Hjalmar and I were completely exhausted with laughter when finally the squirrel made an enormous jump into the water and continued swimming towards the shore. We soon came alongside and stretched out an oar towards it. In a split second it came up the oar across Hjalmar and started the same ceaseless running about as before, outside, inside the gunwale, at a tremendous speed, then it jumped into the water again. We did not interfere any more but let it swim ashore where it entered a pine tree and delivered a long speech telling us without any inferiority complex everything it thought about human creatures like us.

One night I was wandering along the shore with Ruth's fishing rod when I saw a strange movement of the water under some birch trees in front of me. I stopped and watched the movement approach me; it was an otter. He had not yet discovered me and I stood still watching him closely. I was thinking of the beautiful fur and of how well it would suit my wife and there was death in my heart. As he dived I bent down and picked up a big stone and lifted it above my head. Now he was only ten yards away, now six, now four - let go! Off went the stone and missed. The otter disappeared and a wave shot like a torpedo off shore upon the shallow water. Forty yards away the otter came to the surface, turned toward me and lay there inspecting me closely with his two small black eyes. I could read in his face every thought that crossed his mind.

'I wonder what sort of fellow you are. What did you mean with that stone? You did not mean to kill me, did you? How you frightened me! You meant to play with me, didn't you? But you were just a bit too brutal weren't you? I don't trust you yet, so we will have a look at each other first.'

He disappeared again then broke the surface a little nearer to the shore, there was not much of him above the surface just the top of his head with his small dark eyes and his tiny ears then part of his back and tail. His whole appearance was full of curiosity.

'Say fellow, what did you mean? If you want to play I am game for it but don't you try to trick me again.'

There was still some murder in my heart and when he broke surface the third time, ten or twelve yards away, I let another stone go and he was gone. We did not meet any more. I felt I had behaved meanly but there was no use regretting what I had done afterwards.

Knud returned after six days absence and I had a great sense of relief that he was safely back. He had first been to see Seming who had received him with the utmost friendliness and promised to take me across the river Glomma in his rowing boat. On his advice Knud had then continued to Rendalen in order to visit John, who was also an old acquaintance of mine. As John was at the *seter* Knud had an extra 20 miles to bike to meet him. John said he would conduct me across the Rendal Valley. He had also put Knud in touch with a third person, Peder, who would take me across the river Klara. I did not know Peder so John made a 'passport' which would introduce me to him. It was a tiny square of paper with a word written across it. I then cut it irregularly into two pieces. One piece was given to Peder and Knud presented the other to me. When I met Peder we would compare halves thus making sure we had found the right person. Peder had not yet been contacted but John would arrange that and when everything was ready I would receive a signal. I would then have to signal back when I would arrive at the western bank of the River Glomma. From then on everything would be arranged automatically. The meeting places and the hours of meeting were pre-arranged. I only had to await the signal that would mean 'All clear'.

The night after Knud's return I went fishing as usual when I heard a plane approaching. I knew that the paratroopers in the mountains were expecting a drop of supplies. It was a British plane and as I stood there watching it move rapidly eastwards I felt grateful to the British who were our Allies in the war. This plane was to me a sign of the friendship between our people and also a symbol of freedom and justice. Here was the actual proof that our alliance was not mere words. This connection was the life blood of the Norwegian resistance movement and I knew it would grow stronger with every day until it would smash the swastika into pieces and remove it for ever.

The plane soon disappeared over the mountains east of the lake, and I could not see it dropping the parachutes. After a while I heard it moving north, and I knew its job was done. My unknown friends in the mountains had got their supplies.

A few days later Hjalmar came to me and said: "I have had a telephone call informing me that the conditions for angling in the river Glomma are favourable."

The signal had come, I was going to leave. It was now up to me to give the signal when I would start. I asked Hjalmar to phone Seming and tell him he should come on Thursday afternoon with the ordinary 6.00pm train to try his luck fishing. It meant that at 7.00pm that evening Seming would fetch me in his boat at a certain place on the western bank of the river Glomma and take me across.

The day of departure had come, it was a Thursday, a clear warm day with brilliant sunshine. It was quite natural that my friends wanted to say goodbye to me. I was, as usual, sitting on my stone after mid-day when the first boat appeared. I could see it leaving the shore below the farm and crossing the lake south of me. Then it came along the shore on my side and landed near my stone. The visitors were Professor Werenskold, his wife and daughter, my god-daughter Marit. They unfolded a large map and we discussed my route. Apparently the professor wanted to assure himself that I would not miss my way at any point. Mrs. Werenskold gave me a pack of cigarettes and a still more valuable gift, a piece of chocolate. Marit, sweet little thing, enjoyed herself by throwing small stones into the lake and the splashes made her scream with joy. I had to fetch ever bigger stones from the shore and place them on the utmost edge of my stone so that little Marit could thrust them into the lake. I am afraid my friend, the miller's thumb that was living under my stone, found it a rather noisy way of saying goodbye.

The family Werenskold had hardy disappeared when I heard scratching of boots at my shore side and Jørgen appeared smiling all over his good looking face. He handed me a pack of tobacco with a peculiar expression on his face: "Don't mention it, it is next to nothing."

He inspected my boots carefully and said: "Why what a fool I have been not to have thought of this before. You can't go to Sweden like this. Let me have your boots until tonight and I will mend them for you."

I said I could not be without them as I had quite a long way to go through the forest to my tent and I would need them when I was going to pack down all my things. Then Jørgen insisted that he would be at the beach at a certain place at nine that night when I would pass on my way down the lake. He would bring an iron last and some shoe repairer.

Knud was the next to come and we went together to my camping place and he assisted in taking down the tent and packing everything. How everything changed when the tent had been taken away. How barren and miserable the thicket looked. I had not noticed until now that the trees we had erected to construct the thicket had faded, the needles of the small spruces falling off when we touched a branch.

When everything was ready we carried the huge heap of luggage to the shore and Knud rowed across to the farm with it.

The next to come was a diver. How many times had I been hunting for this predatory bird on the lake without being able to get near them? There he came, unaware of me, swimming along the shore straight for my stone. A hundred yards away he dived and I lay down in order not to be observed when he came to the surface again. A splash and there he was hardly 15 yards away, silvery pearls of water dripping from his beak. How beautiful he was in his black and white striped coat, how firm though smooth his velvet garment. His yellow eyes seemed almost phosphorescent against his head of black velvet and his right eye was looking straight in my direction without discovering me. He shook his head, kept rowing forward a few strokes, then suddenly plunged again into the dark water and disappeared, he was a hundred yards away when he reappeared.

The boat below the farm was on the move again. Two white sleeves were reflecting the suns rays. Inga! She brought my luncheon and kept me company for a long time. She told me plainly that she would miss the tent and the secret nocturnal excursions with my food. It had given them such pleasure and such a change in their daily work to plan the trips and collect the things they were to bring to me. Now she was bringing me all I needed for my further journey: pork, butter, bread, cheese, oats and other provisions. She had stolen the oats from an old acquaintance of mine, Miss Reitan, who was an elderly zoologist of the Hans Speeman school. Miss Reitan had no idea where her Danish oats went. I confessed later on and she has forgiven both Inga and myself. Inga also brought me another gift, an old fishing rod which I was going to carry as camouflage on my journey, hoping that people would think I was an angler. That rod had been at the farm for at least 50 years and was a bit old fashioned, I never used it.

Inga was going to collect her cows in the forest so I kissed her goodbye and felt sorry because I was going away, sorry also because I was unable to thank her as I wanted to. I never could.

Knud returned at seven, he had planned on rowing along the western bank of the lake but Ruth and Hjalmar had insisted that we should come across so that they would be able to say goodbye to me. What a lot of goodbyes!

Knud brought my dinner which Inga had prepared, it was a substantial meal because I would have a strenuous walk before me. I wondered whether I would be able to walk at all when I had swallowed that dinner! Tomato soup, pork fried in sour cream with almond potatoes followed by hot blueberry pancakes, I may add that Inga is an expert cook. Knud was rowing while I was eating.

There they were, Ruth and Hjalmar. We all sat down on an old pine root. None of us could find anything to talk about. Hjalmar gave me a pack of tobacco and Ruth had cigarettes for me. I suddenly remembered I had lots of money, and I said to Hjalmar I would pay for my sojourn. Hjalmar shook his head decisively.

"By no means, you have been my guest and I am happy I have been able to shelter you."

Later on Knud told me that he too tried to pay for his stay. He had been living at the farm for quite a number of days then and what was Hjalmar's reply to my brother?

"Nonsense, you have been so kind to Sven that I can't take any payment from you!"

I am happy to know that there are still parts, many parts of Norway, in which morale and true friendship between people have not been destroyed by the German occupation.

Finally there was Jørgen, as Knud was rowing me across the lake to the last meeting place, I discovered that among the things he had brought for my dinner there was a big jar which he had forgotten to show me. It was full of *multekrem*. That word cannot be translated into English as *multe* berries do not grow in Great Britain. They are the favourite berries of all Norwegians, (*Rubus charmaemorus*). They are yellow, almost transparent, a shape much like raspberries, soft and full of sweet juice with a taste of sunshine and they grow in the mountain marshes. Britons do not like them. *Multekrem* is a thick, sweet, whipped cream mixed with *multe* berries. It tastes like heaven and you can't stop eating it until you are full up just behind your eyes. Inga had prepared this one from especially thick cream in honour of my departure.

When I discovered that jar I just said to Knud, "Go on pulling your oars you lazy fellow."

Thus we came to the meeting place with Jørgen. He was there between the boulders of the bank with his iron last, a hammer and some shoe repairer. I kept on eating *multekrem* while he pulled off my boots, one after the other, and mended them. Another goodbye to a good friend and I rolled back into the boat. Knud pulled on the oars again and we made for the lower part of the lake.

There is not much to be said about our departure. Knud was looking lonely in his boat when he was rowing back to the farm and I felt lonely too, standing on the beach with a lump in my throat, waving my hand until Knud was out of sight. I started to walk at 11.00pm. Little did I imagine then, that eight days later, I was to meet Knud and his family in the Norwegian Central Refugee Camp in Sweden.

Chapter 18

ONWARDS TO SWEDEN

The weeks of laziness and too much eating had made me soft, physically and mentally. I feel ashamed now when thinking of it. This was the starving, poor occupied Norway. As an outlaw I had been living too well, had too much to eat and too many substantial meals. I had nearly grown fat. At the very same time my country fellows in the city had no meat at all and a very limited supply of poor fish. They were short of potatoes, and they had half a pint of bluish skimmed milk every week. My own mother, aged 74, had that ration. It was iniquitous, I admit that. The country people had far more and far better. They had a compulsory delivery of eggs, hay, corn, potatoes, meat and milk, or, when their farms were remotely situated butter. They sabotaged the deliveries and produced all possible excuses for not being able to deliver their compulsory quantities. They knew their fellow countrymen in the cities were on the edge of starvation. Why then did they not deliver?

The answer was a simple one, the Germans had full control of the dairies and butcheries. Every farmer knew that everything he delivered would be to the benefit of the Germans, and that no Norwegian would ever receive an ounce of what he delivered. Honest farmers preferred to sell or give away their products to their friends, acquaintances, or their old customers. Lots of the produce also found its way into the black market and was paid for with fancy prices. Money was plentiful, wares rare. The situation in Norway was entirely different from that of Great Britain. Britain was a nation at war, the nation was all one people and all produce was to the benefit of the whole nation. To sell on the black market was a crime. In Norway the black market, seen from a patriotic point of view, was 'legal', and the compulsory delivery of farm products from the same point of view was a crime.

This peculiar distribution of rural products in Norway was not 'just', as it was purely a matter of chance who had the wares and who did not. People who were acquainted with farmers and had sufficient money got preference over those who had no acquaintance in the country or were unable to pay the requested prices. Honest farmers were aware of that and tried to help whenever they were able. Profiteers sold their produce to those who were able to pay the price, i.e. in the black market. Thus there arose two outlets, a 'legal' and an 'illegal' black market. During the occupation there was scarcely ever a full understanding between the city and the rural population but it could hardly be otherwise. Every man is his own next of kin. The war in Norway was not a visible one and many people did not, or could not understand that a war was on, simply because nothing happened in their district. It is only human to put one's own needs first, and it is hardly just to reproach the farmers because they had a higher standard of living during the occupation. The main thing was to prevent wares from being brought into channels which led to the occupiers.

It was because of this peculiar situation that I was now near to the point of being over fed, and at the same time I had exercised little, my physical condition was poor and walking felt strenuous.

My way led across two small valleys. In the middle of the night it was now so dark that I had difficulty in seeing my path. The first valley was very overgrown with a dense vegetation of bushes, grass and flowers, the next was full of rocks and boulders, with water in between. In the soft darkness I made very slow progress but finally, at dawn, I found myself in the free open mountains.

Lake Atnasjøen had disappeared, in the forest below I could only see the S-shape groove marking its position. Across that groove the Rondane Mountains arose, some of them still with white glaciers. South of them was an enormous mountain plain at an altitude of about three thousand feet. North-east of me, on the eastern side of the lake rose a sharp mountain peak, the Solenkletten, forming a dark silhouette against the clear greenish sky. Soon the sun would rise behind it.

In front of me, to the east, were the mountains I was to cross, rising to 4,000 feet. Somewhere past the highest edge was my target for the night, a small timber hut. Seming had sent me the key, an enormous piece of iron weighing at least a pound.

I was now in the land of the paratroopers, my unknown friends. I might meet some of them if they happened to be on the move tonight or I might happen to see their camp but most likely I would see nothing at all.

Just before the sun rose the colours of the landscape changed from dark green into bluish green. The grass, the junipers, the willow bushes, the heather were all bluish green but shading in various strengths of colour. The pine forest far below me in the main valley was nearly black, on a background of yellowish grey reindeer moss but even the dark pines had a touch of bluish green. The colours looked so supernatural that I had the feeling that I had been put into a painting by some mad artist.

The hut was situated just below one of the highest peaks of the district. Some sheep had made themselves comfortable in front of the door where there was a square of sand and I drove them off. In front of the hut was a great flat mountain plain, sloping very slowly to the south-east. A deep, long groove bordered with black forest marked the Glomma Valley where tomorrow night I was going to meet Seming. On the other side of the groove was a row of long, low, even mountains as far as my eye could reach. Perhaps the most distant of them were in Sweden, I could not decide if they were. Only one high, lone mountain rose out of all the plains, the Rendalssølen, rising to 5,300 feet. I would have to pass somewhere near it or perhaps across it. I had plenty of time until I was going to meet Seming. Purposely I started very early because I was out of condition and knew I would get tired. As a matter of fact I was nearly exhausted when I found the hut after only 15 miles of walking. What a shame I said to myself. I would now rest for 24 hours and I went to bed at six in the morning after having made up my mind to sleep for at least twelve hours without interruption.

I had hardly laid down on the bench when I heard

some sheep approaching, their bells ringing in a most irritating manner. Of course they were returning to that patch of dry sand in front of the door. One of them was apparently suffering from lice or scab and was incessantly rubbing its side against the corner of the hut. Its bell finally sounded as if it were in my head. I believe I had to run out, only dressed in pants, at least ten times that day to drive the sheep away. Every time they returned and made themselves comfortable and myself uncomfortable until finally I fell asleep from exhaustion.

In spite of all the disturbance I slept most of the day and the following night until I finally awoke to an unfamiliar sound. The sheep had long since disappeared and something or someone was scratching on the wall of my hut. I thought it was an ermine so I sneaked out, still in underpants, peeped around the corner and found myself facing a squirrel. I need not say that both of us were surprised. Where had the squirrel come from? The nearest forest was at least ten miles away. Not a tree, not even a bush could be seen from here. I left the door open and invited my new friend to a meal inside and chased him towards the open door but he just ran over it and continued around the corner. Thus we kept running round the hut for a long time, I in pants repeating the invitation for a meal, the squirrel declining and leaping over the door every time he passed it. Finally I gave up and placed a piece of bread in a fissure of the timber wall and retired.

At four the next morning I heard the sheep returning from the mountains above. I had forgotten about the squirrel but the moment the sheep rounded the corner of the hut I heard an exclamation from the squirrel, a scratching of tiny claws on the wall and at the same time the sound of galloping sheep and bells disappearing in the distance. When I peeped out the squirrel had disappeared and the sheep were moving rapidly back into the mountains. Their fright had been reciprocal and neither sheep or squirrel returned.

I left at six that same morning and at noon I had the mountain plain behind me and reached the outskirts of the forest which was sloping down to the Glomma River. The big river formed a mighty silver band below me, winding through the broad open valley and through what seemed to be an endless forest. Just occasionally I could see small green open patches in the forest, the farms. Just below me on the other side of the river was Seming's farm, consisting of a low broad, white painted main building, an enormous red painted barn with a clock tower as is the custom in bigger farms in this part of the country, and some other buildings. Wide, pretty meadows surrounded the farm and an avenue of old trees of some sort led from the main road through the meadows to the main building.

People were working in the fields and the sound of the hay cutter extended right up to me. I could see it being pulled by two horses. A cold breeze had been blowing in the mountains but there was no wind at all in the forest, the sun was shining, and it was a lovely summer day.

A cool, clear creek was running through the deep shade of the dense forest near the main river. I undressed and had a bathe but a quick one as the mosquitoes found the same shade a suitable abode.

Serning was late. I became afraid that he had forgotten me, but at nine he entered his boat and pushed it across the river with a long stick, standing erect in the stern. He greeted me heartily and told me he had not been able to get away before because his people had been working in the fields. After the crossing we were to go to a remote and empty barn where his wife would join us and bring some dinner for me.

Inside the big barn we constructed a bench with some planks and made ourselves comfortable. We talked about my further journey. Seming also provided me with some literature. He had some pamphlets that had been dropped from an Allied plane. There was news from the battle fronts and photographs of our King, the Norwegian Government and Norwegian warships and a personal letter from King Haakon to all Home-front men and women, pictures and descriptions of our merchant fleet that had played such an important part in the war. There were pictures and stories about our air force, our fighters who had fought bravely over France on D-Day, and our Coastal Command, among them the new big Sunderlands which frequently patrolled our long coast. The Catilinas and good old 'Vingtor', a slow and heavy plane that for more than two years had yielded invaluable service along our coast and had been seen and was known by the entire coastal population.

Greetings from the free Norwegians in Britain and Canada. Thousands of our fellow countrymen were fighting, some at sea, some in the air, now in their fifth year of exile. They were playing an active and audacious part in the liberation of our country. There was the story of one of our motor tankers that had crossed the Atlantic 43 times and carried more than

8,000,000 tons of high octane gasolene across to Europe, sufficient for 1,000 bomber raids on Berlin.

We had heard about this before, mostly in broadcast news from London but here were photographs and descriptions in small pamphlets, lined with the Norwegian flag, dropped by our own or allied planes in the centre of our occupied country. It had all suddenly become so close at hand. It was an overwhelming feeling and I felt so grateful to all those who were risking their lives every day to secure the great and final victory and the liberation of Norway. Amidst them was King Haakon, our symbol of freedom, our symbol of the coming victory. During the invasion he had been pursued by the Germans for two months throughout Norway, from Oslo to Tromsø. He had been exposed to bombings, to machine guns and fires and had stood up to it all without bending. Now he formed the natural centre of the free and fighting Norway. His broadcast speeches were 'illegally' heard by most Norwegians at home and had encouraged them during the dark times that had passed. He had shown us the way to go during those hard years and now he was showing us the way to victory and liberation. One day he would return, his ship would come up the Oslo fjord, small boats and vessels, hundreds and thousands of them would line his route to the capital. Thousands of boys and girls, men and women, would sing the National Anthem and wave their flags as he passed by. The hills on both sides of the fjord would be clad in their fairest green, the blue, white and red flags would wave in the gentle breeze and he would drive to the royal palace through an enthusiastic crowd. People would gather from all parts of the country to see him back. What a great day it would be!

Sitting in the dark barn, Seming and I were talking about all this. We felt it was worth living and fighting for King and freedom. Were not these summer days of 1944 among the greatest days of the history of the world when four-fifths of all peoples were united in fighting Hitlerism in order to secure the human rights of mankind? Would it ever happen again that all nations would unite like this acting like one people against one mutual foe?

These days Hitler was sending his V-weapons against southern England in order to cause fear and depression. The doodlebugs caused the British nation to stand up more firmly than ever before and work like devils to beat the Huns. Courage, not fear, was their answer to Hitler.

At the same time a million Britons, Australians, Canadians, Africans, Americans, French, Poles, Yugoslavs, Belgians, Dutch, etc., were invading the European continent, every day gaining ground from the retreating Germans. The youth of Norway were forming a firm front against the 'National Labour Service', refusing to work for the Germans, leaving their homes by the thousand to avoid giving a hand to Hitlerism. A great part of the Norwegian nation started understanding why we were fighting and what we were fighting for. Those who had been indifferent, those who had had no understanding that the war was on, those who had been inactive, all united and formed a strong front against tyranny.

They were great days and I felt sorrow that I had to leave Norway just when so much was happening. Such days would never come back.

*

Steps were heard outside the barn; Mrs. Seming came in carrying a big basket containing a delicious dinner and a bottle of beer. An hour went by then I had to leave if I was to be able to reach the next meeting place in the course of the three hours I had left.

Seming went with me across the fields in the twilight explaining how I would find my way through the forest to the place where I was going to meet John. He had telephoned John telling him he would send a parcel with the bus this afternoon. At two o'clock John would be at a disused saw mill in the forest 300 yards south of Lake Harsjøen at the river Horrena, and would guide me across the Rendalen Valley. I would have to follow a path uphill for about two miles until it crossed a small creek. Another path would cross it there and I must turn to the left through the forest until reaching some *seters*, then walk straight east until I met the river Horrena and the meeting place would be close at hand. It sounded easy and I calculated I would be at the meeting place at about 1.30.

It was dark when I met the creek and I was hardly able to distinguish the crossing path. A dense fog swept between the trees and it was raining, I lost my path immediately and was glad I had a map and a compass with a luminous dial. I sat down on the stump of an old tree studying the map by the means of some matches and I found I would have to pass between some lakelets straight east of me, then continue east by south where I would probably find the *seter* pastures. It is quite easy to see one's course on a map but not quite so easy to follow it in darkness through a dense forest when bushes and branches make you stumble twice a minute, when it is raining and a dense fog prevents you from seeing more than 50 yards ahead. It would be OK if I had plenty of time but it was already past midnight and I had to be at the old sawmill at two sharp, if I wanted to cross the Rendalen Valley before people got out of their beds. Every now and then I had to look at the map and compare with the landscape and the compass and every time I found that the rain and the moisture from my damp clothes were dissolving the map.

I had 40 minutes left when I came to a marsh the width of which I could not judge. For a moment I hesitated then plunged into it, determined to get across however difficult it may be. It might waste too much time to go around it and that would also bring me out of my due course. I soon lost contact with the forest and could see nothing around me but the wet marsh which never seemed to come to an end. I walked on like the devil, my feet sank into the deep moss, my boots were filled with water, rain and sweat ran from my face and my hair down my neck and mosquitoes were swarming around me.

Suddenly there was no marsh any more, I had come to the sandy shore of a lake but because of the mist I could not see across it - I judged it to be Lake Harsjøen.

What luck! After a few minutes I was at the outlet and 300 yards due south brought me to the old sawmill. A saw bench and some battered shanties was all that was left. I dropped down on the saw bench and looked at my watch. Two o'clock sharp. I felt a faint breeze cooling my face and everything had suddenly changed from a hard, disagreeable struggle into mere happiness. I felt that the consequences of laziness and too high a standard of life at Lake Atnasjøen had disappeared. I was strong and fit, I could again sustain some hardships. The faint glow of a cigarette 20 yards away attracted my attention. I went up to that glow addressing it: "Hello John".

A strong hand grasped mine firmly.

John was a tall man of about 30, with a sharp clean-cut face and dark serious looking eyes. He was a farmer and had just taken over from his father. I knew both of them from a period of five to ten years ago, when I used to spend a couple of weeks late in the autumn in the Rendalen Mountains on trout investigations. They came from a very old Rendalen family, the eldest son had inherited the farm from his father for at least four centuries. They were a strong independent people, proud of their ancestors and of their farm. They were of good reputation too, and theirs was one of the oldest and biggest farms in the valley.

We were going to that farm. John led me by a narrow road to the main road. He had his bicycle there and explained to me how I could take some short cuts across the fields and across the southern bridge, which was not guarded. He left me as he wanted to ride directly to the farm in order to have a meal ready for me when I arrived on foot later on.

It had ceased raining and the fog was drifting away, shrinking to small patches which by and by disappeared. I had some six or seven miles to walk, mostly down hill, and had a brilliant view of the valley as I walked down the side of it.

It was four in the morning when I passed through the gate which led up to John's farm. I had been ordered to go straight in without knocking at the door. As I entered from the farmyard by the back door I came into a huge sitting room that dated from 1530. It had been built from heavy pine timber. The southern wall had two wide low windows from which the whole southern part of the valley could be seen. Between them was an old clock. The eastern and western walls were covered with large cupboards with painted inscriptions. The northern wall was open and led into the enormous kitchen with a huge iron cooking stove.

A tall well-built girl was standing at the stove. As I entered I could see only her back with broad, strong shoulders and her thick, golden hair. She was his sister. John introduced me as Mr. Jacobsen. The meal she was preparing consisted of golden pink fleshed trout from Lake Missjøen where, in previous years I had investigated the stock of fish. It was an old custom in the valley that trout from this particular lake should be cooked without salt. After being boiled they are put into a jar, the broth is then salted and poured several times over the fish which are then ready to serve.

Thus prepared the trout obtain a special taste which is particular to Missjø trout. It is counted as the finest course they are able to serve and I understood that John wanted to show me the favour of serving me this special meal before I continued on my journey.

Apart from a few hours' rest at the Glomma River I had now had 22 hours hard walking and felt very tired. John told me he had arranged with his mother that I should rest in the *seter* belonging to the farm. He had also arranged with Peder that I would meet him tonight at 11.30pm near the Klara River. I started calculating, it was 20 miles to the *seter* and another 20 miles to where I was going to meet Peder. It would be 5.30 when I had finished eating. Forty miles and 18 hours to cover them and have a rest at the *seter* was not very much when taking into consideration that I had had more than 30 miles heavy marching behind me and was now very tired. How I was longing for a bed and how nice it would be to lie down and stretch my tired feet but there was little help in thinking of it. I had to go on.

I bade goodbye to John and his sister and made for the *seter*. John lent me his bicycle as I could now follow the road which led straight up to the *seter*.

The road wound through a dense pine forest up the steep and high side of the valley. I had to ascend nearly 2,000 feet and the bicycle felt heavy like lead as I pushed it up the hills.

I knew every turn of the road and every hill, every little spring and creek I was passing but I could not remember that the road had ever been so far or long before. When finally I passed the last hill and had the open mountain plain ahead of me I could make little use of the bicycle as the road had recently been gravelled. Bicycling and walking felt equally heavy but finally I reached the *seter* and knocked at the door.

I had never met John's mother before and introduced myself as Mr. Jacobsen, a brother of Mr. Jacobsen who was here last week. I also brought a letter from John, which apparently told her not to ask any questions, but to give Mr. Jacobsen food and a bed. John's mother did everything to make me feel comfortable. Quite unexpectedly, however, her husband entered. I had met him before and as I was introduced as Mr. Jacobsen he gave me a look full of suspicion and remarked drily he thought he might have seen me before. As he had not been told not to ask questions, he asked a lot, and did not seem to notice the desperate signs of his wife. I was happy I had my old fishing rod as a suitable excuse for telling him I was going to try my fishing luck in the Mistra River, which I had heard should be an excellent trout stream.

It was close to ten o'clock when finally John's mother showed me a small tidy bedroom. A good fire was burning in the tiny iron stove and I fell asleep before I had got all my clothes off after having asked John's mother to call me at three o'clock.

At four I was on my way again, my right foot had started aching, the ankle joint was stiff and swollen, probably from over strain. I soon left the road and made straight for a mountain pass in the Sølen Mountains. The Sølen is the highest mountain in eastern Norway, the highest peak is 5,300 ft. and the pass is 4,000 ft. These parts were long the home of the wild reindeer; Rendalen means the Reindeer Valley. In many places there may still be found traces of old reindeer traps, small narrow pits placed in strategic places where the reindeer used to pass. The traps were mostly covered with branches and moss, sometimes also a low stone wall was built between them in order to lead the deer into the traps. Such traps were very valuable and it has happened that when a farm was going to be shared between a farmer's sons, the eldest son preferred to choose the reindeer traps in the mountains to the farm in the valley.

By the beginning of the 20th century the reindeer had become extinct in the Rendalen Mountains but were later re-introduced and at present they numbered some thousands.

As I approached the pass a cold wind started blowing from the wild peaks and a wet fog swept the mountainside. I got wet on my left side which was turned to the wind but kept dry on my right.

In former days a great part of the traffic between eastern Norway and Sweden went through this pass. Today there is only a hardly visible path at intervals marked with cairns.

On the Northern slope of the pass are numerous old reindeer traps. They were forbidden by law 200 years ago and they were ordered to be filled and levelled. Probably there was insufficient control as most of the pits are as fully fit for use today as they were 200 years ago. A low wall extended between them and 100 yards further down was part of an old round hut built of stones. This hut must have been a *bogastalle* from which the hunters loosed their arrows against the reindeer when they came through the pass.

On the southern slope of the pass is a lake which several years ago I tried to stock with trout fry. Nobody has seen any fish there since so my attempt has probably been unsuccessful.

It started raining heavily and the wind came from the north. I had to use the compass as I could not see very far. The direction John gave me was that I should find a lake called Aursjøen. I would also find a hut there. A distinct path would lead from the hut across the hills east of it and at 11.30pm I would meet Peder on the southern slope of the hills just where the path met with the forest.

After having crossed several marshes I found Aursjøen alright but where was the hut? John had told me he had never been there and he did not know where the hut was but he thought the path would lead north of the Aursjøvola Mountain, just east of the lake. The hut would most probably be on the eastern side of it. I headed for that and found the eastern side was covered with a dense bush forest, mostly consisting of low birches. I forced my way through them, searching every little bay of the lake and every little valley and hill for the hut but could find no sign of it. Could I take the chance of going straight for the northern side of the Aursjøvola Mountain hoping to find the path there?

It was past ten already and the thought tempted me but if the path led south of Aursjøvola, what then? I would not meet Peder and I would not get across the Klara tonight. I might have to depend on people whom I could not trust. I could not take such a risk, I had to find the hut. The eastern side seemed hopeless and it was almost completely dark already. I turned round, forced my way back through the wet bushes and finally found a path leading south along the western bank of the lake. At eleven o'clock I found a hut at the southern end, close to the outlet of the lake, and there was the path.

It took me only half-an-hour to cross the hills and soon I could see the Klara River through the rain far below me.

A man came up to me. He was dressed according to the description Knud had given me, in a grey sporting suit and soft hat, carrying a walking stick. Poor man, he was completely soaked by the rain. He carried a raincoat over his arm but he had not put it on in order not to spoil the description! It was 11.30 sharp.

We said good evening to each other and stopped for a chat as wanderers used to do when they met in the mountains. I opened up my cigarette container and offered the man a cigarette. On top of the cigarettes was the little piece of paper which Knud had given me and which should correspond and match up with the piece sent to Peder. The man took from a pocket the counterpart and studied both the slips solemnly. Then he looked up and said: "I see you are the right person," upon which he turned and led the way down to the river.

Peder told me that besides the farm he had a summer pension. German border guards had sequestered two of the rooms which they used every now and then. Formally he had made friends with the guards but sometimes he went silently away by night to assist refugees. As for the pension the guests nowadays were mostly quislings as they were the only people who were trusted well enough by the Germans to be given permission to go to the eastern boundary zone. Just now a family were his guests and when he described them there could be no doubt this family was formerly among my closest friends. The head of the family was a bit nervous and had been visited by

German officers a few days after the invasion because of his special technical knowledge which they wanted to take advantage of for a special purpose. He had been so scared that he became a member of the Nazi party. His wife joined him and both of them soon became active members of the party. They were my only friends to join the Nazi party.

"Just as I left home," said Peder, "he went to the river with his rod."

"I'll tell you how he was dressed," said I "because I know his habits fairly well. As it was raining he wore heavy rubber boots and a long oilskin coat, which was buttoned carefully and he wore gloves, a scarf around his neck, and a sou'wester."

Peder looked at me in astonishment.

"Indeed you know him well," he said. "In case he should still be at the river I have brought two long bamboo rods as camouflage. When we are crossing keep an eye to the eastern bank. My wife will tie a white handkerchief to a bush if there is any danger."

There was no handkerchief and the crossing was easy.

"And now," said Peder, "what will you do? Do you want to go to the border tonight? There are 22 miles left and if you want to go I will be at your disposal as a guide, or do you need a rest?

I told him I was very tired and my right foot was hurt so I would prefer a rest.

"I am sorry I can't take you to my home but the guards may come or they may not. Anyway you are not safe there as someone might see you."

He told me he had a neighbour whom he thought he might trust but he would prefer to keep him out of it.

"I need no bed or house. A shelter against the rain is sufficient for me. An old barn or a shanty of some sort will do," I told him.

"Well then, there is a sort of shanty fifty yards away from the main road. It is only a roof on four poles, no walls at all but it is only two hundred yards from my farm, I'll fetch you a reindeer skin to rest upon and an old fur coat as a cover. There is only one thing about that shelter, the border guards are passing by the road all night long in their vehicles but you should be perfectly safe there as they never leave the road."

"OK. I'll sleep there."

The roof was tight and kept the rain out. Peder brought the things he had promised and I tried to make myself comfortable on a heap of planks on the 'floor'. As I was thoroughly soaked with the rain I undressed and distributed all my wet clothes on the planks and then settled to sleep with my pistol close at hand.

I was too tired to fall asleep at once and as I was lying there, only sheltered from above, my lodging was suddenly lit up by the headlights of a vehicle that was passing by. There was a bend just south of my shelter and the headlights from all cars passing north through the valley would consequently light up my shanty. Well, I was too tired to bother about it and I trusted Peder's words when he said that no one would examine the shanty. I turned my back to the road and was soon sound asleep, only now and then disturbed by passing cars and their lights.

I was awoken by the noise of steps outside, one person only and the steps were normal. It could be nobody but Peder. Germans would come in numbers and they would surround the shanty from all sides and call out orders to each other.

As I was still tired I kept my eyes closed until Peder said good morning. He carried a kettle filled with hot coffee substitute.

"You are not very nervous", he said.

I told him that I had trusted his word that nobody would examine the shanty. If I had not trusted him I could not have gone to sleep here at all. Which was, of course, quite right.

It was eight in the morning. We were going to start at eleven and Peder would guide me across the next valley, 15 miles away. He thought I would easily find my way to the boundary from there. There was only one remote *seter* near the border and as to the boundary itself it was never guarded. The Germans only sent a patrol now and then to control the remote places and they always went four or five together as they had discovered that it was too risky to go alone or in couples.

My clothes had not dried at all during the night and

I had to pull them on as they were. They felt like wet bandages in the beginning but I soon got used to it and did not feel cold.

We walked through the forest all day, having to control our course by means of the compass frequently, as it was foggy. It was dark when we came to the main road of the Engerdal Valley. Peder whispered to me to hide, then he walked cautiously down to the road, looking in both directions. There was a bridge across the main river just below us and it was probably guarded. Then Peder waved 'all clear' to me and we both ran across the road into the bushes on the other side. We went upwards along the river until we came to a dam where a narrow bridge led across, then we crossed by the bridge. We had seen nobody and nobody had seen us.

When we parted in the dense forest I asked Peder if he would feel offended if I gave him some money. When he said, "Do as you like," I gave him 300 kroner, thanked him for what he had done for me and bade him goodbye.

I had been looking forward to this night for a long time. Yes, I was going to cross the border between Norway and Sweden, from war to neutrality, from slavery into freedom, from terrorism to justice. I had been thinking of a well guarded boundary with German armed guards at certain intervals or small bodies of soldiers patrolling the border. I knew now that this was not true. In fact the border itself was not regularly guarded only the roads leading to it or along it. Now and then a patrol consisting of five or ten soldiers would visit remote farms or *seters* along the border line or inspect less used paths near it.

A soldier would never dare go alone in such remote places. Altogether there was only a very small risk that I would meet a guard.

The weather was as I had hoped for: It was foggy, drizzling and dark. My way led upwards through the forest rising to about a thousand feet. Then I would meet some marshes before I got into the barren mountains. Then - well I had my compass and a fairly good map, I thought I would find my way easily. Although I knew there was little danger of meeting Germans I could not help feeling a bit excited and as I ascended the slope through the forest my right hand often found its way into the pocket where I had my heavy pistol.

Judging from the map it would be easy to find the first hill of the open mountains. I estimated the whole march to the border would take me about three hours. I would be in Sweden at three in the morning. The first hill was easily found, it was sloping vaguely uphill but the fog was so dense that I could hardly see fifty yards in front of me and very soon I lost the sense of what was uphill and what was downhill. Everything was a grey mass. Every now and then I had to look at the map. The air was wet, my hands were wet, my clothes were even more so, and the map got wet also, and soon it dissolved into some kind of cereal.

I was afraid my pistol would have an influence upon the compass so at intervals I left the pistol on a stone and controlled the compass at some distance from it. Then I continued, compass in hand. It was so dark that I could only distinguish the particulars of the map by means of matches and I burnt nearly a box of matches that night.

I found the small stream I was searching for. It was running to the south and my course was due east. North of me now I would have a lake from which the stream emerged. In front of me I would have a stretch of wet marshes which I must avoid, but a mile south of the lake there should be a strip of dry land across the marshes. Therefore I decided to find the lake then follow the stream due south for a twenty minute walk then turn due east.

I reached the lake but owing to the dense fog I could only see part of the surface not the opposite bank. According to plan, I turned south and walked for 20 minutes then turned east compass in hand. Nature seemed dead around me, there was no wind, no animal to be seen. No bird flew out of the bushes as I made my way through them. No sound except the sucking noise from my own steps. The low willow bushes and junipers were heavy with glittering drops, condensed from the wet fog and when I touched them they unloaded showers of water on my knees and legs. Nasty weather but exactly as I had wanted it.

Oh! No, this must be wrong. There was no dry strip of land, wet moss, wet bushes, wet morass only and as I proceeded my feet sank deeper and deeper into the bog. My walking by and by changed into wading and soon I was knee deep in a watery bog. If only I could see a few hundred yards I might see dry land somewhere. Now I could see nothing but moor and bushes, I had to go back.

A thought struck me, given the lake I had seen was no lake, given that it was only an extended part of the stream too small to be marked on my map. I had to go back, so compass in hand I turned west. It was so dark I could not even find my own footprints in the bog and during my attempts to find them I sank even deeper into the marsh. Finally I was on dry land again, found the creek and started anew searching for the lake. After about 20 minutes walk I found it alright as I had seen it before but this time I decided to examine the extent of it.

It took me about 30 seconds to go around it to the opposite bank. It was no lake, only a pool. How that fog can betray! A further ten minutes brought me to the real lake this time there was no doubt. I marched along the bank, 100 yards, 500 yards, and still it was extending to the east, no doubt this was the one.

An hour lost, it vexed me, but as a matter of fact it was unimportant. Now twenty minutes south, then east, and I found the passage across the moor. The border which had for a while seemed so distant was once again within reach but what a landscape, morass, bushes and bog again. I would now have to pass between two lakes but I did not see them. I must have passed close to one of them because I found, under some bushes, a pair of oars belonging to a rowing boat, and I deemed it a satisfactory sign that my course was correct.

I was on the barren mountains again and somewhere, hidden in the fog ahead of me, was a small *seter*, the last dangerous point of my route. I found a path marked with small cairns and walked on lustily. On and on. The weather was improving and it was soon full daylight again.

Five o'clock, I should have passed the *seter* by now. I walked and walked without seeing it, nor did I see any sign of the border. Then - there was the *seter.*

No sign of people and no sign of danger. 5,000 yards east would be the boundary.

I made my way through the bushes a good distance away from the *seter* in order not to awaken any possible dog, found a path again and went on towards the east. My path was sloping down slowly and I was soon in the forest again. This had to be Sweden there was no other possibility. I must have crossed the border without noticing it.

I found a pine with bushy branches and flung my pistol between them. I wanted the Swedish border guards to find me unarmed.

The forest grew more dense as I went on but suddenly it opened into wide meadows. A shallow lake was lying ahead of me it was bordered by green rushes. Some ducks were swimming peacefully at the mouth of a small river and there, 100 yards away from where I came out of the forest, was a low *seter* house surrounded by barns and cow stables. A Swedish *seter*!

I went up to it and knocked at the door. The door to freedom.

Epilogue

The Swedish authorities were accustomed to refugees from Norway escaping across their borders and my father was granted asylum after some initial investigation as to his true identity.* He spent a few weeks at a refugee camp in Sweden where he was reunited with his brother Knud who had also fled with his family. In September 1944 he flew to England to join the Norwegian Ministry of Agriculture with whom he was employed as principal of the Fishery School.

In London he had an audience with King Haakon who liked to receive all who had escaped from the Nazis. He was a dignified and much loved monarch. When he enquired how Sven had escaped, my father replied somewhat cheekily, "Well, that is a secret, your Majesty."

"Quite right", said the King, "I would really much rather talk about the country in general. Do the people want me back? What are the thoughts of ordinary folk?"

Pappa was able to reassure him that the Norwegians longed for his return and most households had a bottle of some sort hidden away to celebrate of his homecoming. That memorable day dawned at last when King Haakon was escorted home by the British Navy. As soon as his ship neared the Norwegian coast, small boats appeared from farms and villages, gathering in numbers all the way up the long Oslo fjord welcoming the King home. My father was with the Government and officials from the ministries on board one of the escorting vessels. Norway was free at last from tyranny and fear.

* Sven adopted several aliases during his work with the Norwegian resistance.

Wednesday 28th July 2004

And so here we were, 60 years later, in Selma's pretty sitting room with the sun pouring in through the window. She had just given us back Pappa's shoes, sung her song and told us about her life and her work with the Norwegian resistance during the war. We were fit and ready to go.

We wanted to see the way Pappa had gone, to follow in his footsteps and to experience a little of the effort it had cost him. It hadn't been possible to walk across the valley from Åndalsnes simply because the track had now disappeared and the forest was too dense to get through. So we started from Isfjorden on a trek that was to take us nearly 200 miles across the mountains to the border with Sweden.

Oddmund Unhjem came with us for the first part to Eikesdal. It took about 20 minutes to reach the foot of the mountain. The drive up the valley was lovely, warm summer sunshine with the trees, especially the silver birches in full bloom. All the way up we followed the course of the river Pappa had walked beside. Oddmund told us that my father had stayed a night or two in a little barn on the side of the track, but there were quite a few and so we were unable to find the right one. We also passed a bridge he had crossed.

Our first climb was hard but we were all feeling fit and keen to get started. It was wonderful to feel the pull on the backs of our legs as we inched our way slowly upwards. I could feel the clear mountain air filling my lungs and the sweat beginning to form on my back under the rucksack. The sun was hot but there was enough breeze to give us energy. The path was steep all the way up and in places we had to hang on to chains that had been slung across to help walkers. Don't look down! Although near the top it was fun to see down into the valley the way we had come. This was truly God's country. There was a beautiful river and waterfall hurtling down the mountainside to our left, how clear the water was. Then Oddmund showed us a small green patch of grass, high up where we were heading, strangely out of place amidst all the rock and scree, where there were 123 species of flowers growing. Sure enough we found many of them, it was high summer and they were flowering. All the colours so vivid, blues, yellows and pinks, little alpines clinging to the side of the mountain and growing out of crevices and in places with no soil. I wondered how they survive the harsh long winters up here. Then every now and again we would be followed by a small bird, curiously watching us with it's head on one side. We found blueberries, the berries of our childhood, and grabbed a handful to eat. How delicious, although they leave you with a delightfully blue tongue! And always the sound of the waterfall crashing down beside us.

At last, after about two hours we reached the top. The next morning dawned bright and chilly but we were high up and we packed our stuff and set off with Oddmund leading the way. He had warned me that we must stick together as a group otherwise we would be in trouble and could soon lose each other. We stopped for lunch and took our shoes off to dip them in a small ice-cold lake that still had large boulders of snow melting in it. The water was the most amazing azure blue. Oddmund said that the water is now piped off for the people living in the valley below, so it's not a very safe place to swim because of the underwater pipes taking the water out. Not that any of us fancied the freezing cold water!

The sun was high in the sky as we made our way towards a hill that Oddmund said was where Pappa had left the door he had been given to carry when he and his helpers had come this way 60 years earlier in case they encountered any German soldiers up there. Then they could say they were going to build a hut on the mountain. He had left the door lying up there and it had been found and photographed a few years ago. My brother Bertie had to leave us at this point, suffering from a badly swollen knee from an old injury.

We set off again across fairly flat terrain before our long descent into the Eikesdal valley. The view was breathtaking, tiny houses dotted the valley floor below us and on the other side we could see the steep rise of the mountains where several waterfalls were hurtling downwards in a never-ending force of water. We could see the sun glinting on the mountain tops and the occasional patch of snow that never melts. This was the most strenuous part of the whole route. It was a very steep descent, several thousand feet and almost vertical in places where we clung to the vegetation to keep from slipping and with our heavy rucksacks. It was quite a relief when, some two hours later, we reached the green valley floor.

This part of Norway is most spectacular, the mountains rising to nearly 6,000 feet in places. The valley floor is green and fertile with small farms dotted about and a road running from one end to the other. Then there's the Eikesdal fjord, still and smooth and inviting although bitterly cold and crystal clear.

There we met Kristian whose parents, Nikolai and Marit Finset, had hidden Pappa during his escape. A quiet, gentle, retired farmer, Kristian told us he had been ten years old when Pappa arrived at his parent's house and how he was sworn to secrecy. Even children realised that there was danger all around and that they must not talk about things they had seen which could cause great problems for their families with the Nazis.

Over the next nine days we walked through some of the most beautiful countryside, following the route Pappa had taken. He was very much in our thoughts along the way. I kept thinking how lonely he must have been, always keeping an eye out for German soldiers and having to be careful no-one saw him.

On day nine Oliver decided to return home. In the afternoon we set off from Fokstugu in the rain. Crossing loose scree coming out of a ravine, Linda tripped and fell, the weight of her rucksack slamming her face into the rock. Bleeding badly from a cut above her eye and a broken nose, she managed to walk to Grimsdalshytta where she was taken to hospital, leaving Yuli and I on our own. We were now very aware of the danger should one of us have an accident.

I was suffering from severe stomach cramps by the time we reached Nesset where we had warm, soft beds with duvets and some good food. We swam in the black waters of Lake Atna and briefly met Hjalmar's widow. It was good to have a link with Pappa's past again.

For the next few days we walked through bear and wolf country, became lost in bogs and dense forests, waded through rivers, edged our way along narrow mountain paths, sometimes clinging to small trees to stop ourselves falling, and trekked through ancient reindeer passes that Pappa had described. We were bitten by midges and suffered with painfully swollen feet, just as he had. We drank from cold mountain streams, feasted on golden berries that tasted of sunshine and honey, sang and laughed at silly jokes to keep one another going, never doubting that we would make it.

Two and a half weeks after we set out we arrived at a deserted campsite in Engerdal where we pitched our tent for the last time. We were exhausted, had virtually run out of food and could go no further as we had no idea where Pappa had crossed the border. We were some ten kilometres from Sweden. We had come as far as we could.

Before returning to England, Yuli and I felt we needed a conclusion, a closure; something to acknowledge what Pappa had endured and to mark his journey to freedom. We need a ceremony. A small river seemed a fitting place. It was peaceful and quiet, and with the dappled sun on the water we lit candles for the people who had been involved in this extraordinary story. For Pappa's brothers and sisters, especially Iacob who had given his life for the freedom of his countrymen. Then we offered up two pairs of smelly socks as a sacrifice which we burnt in the fire. As we sent the candles down the river, we let Pappa go – his spirit lives on in his beloved Norway and we carry our happy memories of him, his sense of humour and fun, his courage and fortitude throughout his eight week flight and his ultimate battle with cancer that claimed his life at the age of 57. When I think of him and how he used his trick of leaping up into the air on a sapling so as not to leave his footprints for the soldiers to follow, I am reminded of Robert Frost's poem *Birches*.

> Then he flung outward, feet first, with a swish,
> Kicking his way down through the air to the ground.
> So once was I myself a swinger of birches,
> And so I dream of going back to be.
> It's when I'm weary of considerations,
> And life is too much like a pathless wood
> Where your face burns and tickles with the cobwebs
> Broken across it, and one eye is weeping
> From a twig's having lashed across it open.
> I'd like to get away from earth awhile
> And then come back to it and begin over.
> May no fate wilfully misunderstand me
> And half grant what I wish and snatch me away
> Not to return. Earth's the right place for love:
> I don't know where it's likely to go better.
> I'd like to go by climbing a birch tree,
> And climb black branches up a snow-white trunk
> *Toward* heaven, till the tree could bear no more,
> But dipped its top and set me down again.
> That would be good both going and coming back.
> One could do worse than be a swinger of birches.

Pappa would have liked that.

Iacob Sømme

Iacob's Story

Sven Sømme's brother, Iacob, became involved in the build up of the Military Organization (Milorg) of the Norwegian secret resistance movement as early as 1940. Later, he became head of intelligence, developing new methods of espionage and sending important messages by radio to Britain or by courier to Sweden. Iacob Sømme was arrested by the Germans in October 1942, and spent 18 months in prison at Grini outside Oslo. His New Year's Eve speech to his fellow prisoners on the 31st December 1943 became famous. It was full of hope for their future freedom, though he did not himself live to see the end of the war.

Sixty years after the German occupation in 1940-1945, his son Lauritz Sømme recalls the moment at the age of eleven he saw his father in Grini for the last time. The background of Sven and Iacob's work was the determination of the Norwegian people to resist their occupiers. Several groups were founded at an early stage of the occupation and gradually formed into larger organizations, Milorg being one of them. Their objectives were to send information about German installations and activities to the allies in Britain, to prepare for the fight for freedom by receiving weapons from secret air-drops and by carrying out sabotage against the Germans. All this work had to be done in great secrecy. Several thousand men and women were engaged in the resistance movements. If arrested, they risked imprisonment in Norway or German concentration camps or even death, and their families risked persecution.

Sentenced to death

Iacob had been tortured at the Gestapo Headquarters at Victoria Terrasse in Oslo. In a court held by 'SS-und Polizeigericht Nord' on the 17th November 1943, Iacob was sentenced to death by the judge, Hans Latza, who was responsible for a number of death sentences during the occupation. The prosecutor was Karl Denk and defence was given by Dr. Munthendorf. The death sentence was ordered because of continued activities to support a hostile nation. According to the prosecution, Iacob had conducted extensive activities for more than two years, collecting information of importance to the war and making it available to hostile agents.

Iacob had an unknown helper, a man by the name of Sven Dysthe, who played a dual role during the war. As a member of the Norwegian Nazi party, he became acquainted with German officials, and socialized with them. One of his German 'friends' was the judge, Hans Latza. On several occasions Dysthe persuaded the judge to ask for a dismissal of the death sentences. Through the Gerichtsherr Wilhelm Rediess, Latza's request went directly to the Reichskommisar Joseph Terboven, head of the German administration in Norway. In December 1943, Dysthe became involved in the case of Iacob Somme. On a visit to Latza's office in December 1943, he learned that the judge had enormous respect for the prisoner. According to Sven Dysthe, Latza said that he liked Iacob, and, strangely enough it appeared that Iacob also liked the judge, although he had read his sentence. Latza considered Iacob as an exceptionally brave man. Since the accusations against Iacob were very serious, and since he had not betrayed any of his colleagues during interrogation, Latza did not believe that the death sentence could be avoided. However, he was once more willing to appeal for a reprieve to Rediess and Terboven, and expressed some hope that he would succeed. Following this meeting, Dysthe sent a message to Iacob's mother, Helene, and informed her, quite confidentially, that she should not worry about her son's future.

Iacob's mother was allowed to visit him a few times when he was brought to the Gestapo Headquarters in Oslo for interrogation in October 1943. Later that year, believing his sentence had been annulled, she passed the message on to him. Iacob was in a happy mood when he was returned to Grini. The other prisoners were also relieved by the news and celebrated as much as possible, given the circumstances

According to Harald Ulrik Sverdrup-Thygeson, who was Iacob's friend and also a prisoner at Grini, Iacob actually doubted very much that his sentence had been annulled. He also talked with Harald about his ideas for the international regulation of fisheries, only two weeks before his execution. With a pencil, Iacob wrote his testament on paper towels, including the state of his scientific work, which were smuggled out of the prison. After the war, his suggestions for the fisheries were published in December 1945 as a chronicle in the newspaper *Verdens Gang.*

During the night of the 2nd March 1944, the large sleeping quarters where Iacob spent his last days in prison, were woken by German guards. Iacob and six other prisoners were taken away and executed early in the morning at the military camp at Trandem, north of Oslo. His name is found in the memorial at the place of execution.

Grini

Some years after the occupation, Iacob's son Lauritz met another of his fellow prisoners, Per Eivind Fossum, who shared a cell at Grini with Iacob for more than a year. In a cell with only two bunks, a third man was also imprisoned. One of them had to sleep on the floor. During daytime they were allowed to leave the cell for half an hour. Within their restricted world, Iacob developed a programme of activities, including daily walks in circles, gymnastics and talks. The confinement of these three men in such a restricted place was extremely stressful.

Since the Germans could not prove their accusations against him, Per Fossum was eventually released. In fact, he had been engaged in receiving air drops of weapons from British planes in the forests south of Oslo. After his return to freedom he continued the secret distribution of weapons to members of the resistance forces.

Iacob was tortured repeatedly, but according to Fossum the Germans were not really aware of his rank. Under torture, another prisoner had informed the Germans that Iacob was Milorg's head of intelligence.

Late in 1943, Iacob was transferred to a large cell on the fourth floor of the prison building at Grini. The prisoners called it 'the parachute', partly because it was far above the ground and ironically because this was where prisoners sentenced to death spent their last days. The large hall was originally designed for gymnastics, but was turned into a cell for 77 prisoners. According to some of them, the time was passed with talks and lectures given by the inmates. Iacob talked about his work on trout and the policy of Norwegian fisheries.

Secret work

In Milorg and the so-called Home Front, which later became the main resistance organization, it was important that members did not know each other's identity. In this way their names could not be revealed to the Germans, even under torture. The members operated under fictitious names, but even then, complete secrecy was not always possible. This secrecy continued even after the war, making it difficult to discover details of all the activities of the different participants, particularly those who did not survive. For this reason, very few details are known of Iacob's work, except for fragmentary information published in some of the books immediately after the war. His activities appear to have been quite extensive however. His information had to be sent to London, and Iacob was in charge of a secret radio station through which messages were transmitted.

His arrest resulted in problems for the radio station, and some of Milorg's members had to go into hiding.

At Grini, Iacob told Per Fossum about some of his espionage work. Iacob organized the collection of photographs of various German military installations, including the harbour of Oslo. He also received photographs of German harbours from sailors who had been to Germany. These were sent via Sweden to the allied forces in England by different methods. Iacob discovered that when the 36mm film was kept moist after development, the gelatine layer with the pictures could be carefully removed with a razor blade, leaving only a thin membrane which could be rolled into a ball and was easy to hide for the couriers. When the balls were later soaked in water, the gelatine unfolded and the picture could be copied and enlarged. One of the couriers to Sweden had a hollow molar tooth. When the top was removed, there was room for the tiny gelatine balls. With the crown of the tooth replaced, it was quite impossible for the balls to be found, even if the courier was caught at the border by German guards.

The heavy water at Rjukan

The Norsk Hydro factories at Rjukan, situated in a steep valley in the mountainous central area of Norway, became very important during the war. They were the world's only source of heavy water production, necessary for the production of atomic bombs. The Germans did not possess the equipment in their own country. In order to prevent the development of atomic weapons in Germany, the plants became an important target for the allied forces.

Plans to demolish or bomb the factories started in 1942, and Iacob Sømme became involved in the early phase of the planning. Norwegian and British commandoes were supposed to sabotage the factories after landing at the lakes in the mountains. In the autumn of 1942 Iacob was in secret contact with a man at Rjukan to receive information about the thickness of ice at the lakes. The man should call Iacob over the telephone, which could be overheard by the Germans, and tell him the sizes of the trout he had caught. The length of trout corresponded to the thickness of the ice. When Iacob was arrested in October, other members of Milorg continued this work, including transmission of messages to England by radio.

The events that followed were very dramatic. In February 1943, Norwegian commandoes managed to blow up part of the factory, and the production of heavy water was delayed. Their heroic work later formed the basis of the film *The Heroes of Telemark*. The Germans managed to repair the factory, but decided to move the production to Germany. The transport had to go by rail, and the train crossed Lake Tinnsjø on a ferry. On the 20th February, 1944, Norwegian saboteurs managed to sink the ferry at the deepest part of the lake. The heavy water was lost, and the Germans never succeeded in making an atomic bomb.

Afterwards, rumours spread that Iacob and the other six prisoners from Grini had been executed as reprisals for the sabotage at Tinnsjø.

*

The New Year's Eve speech given by Iacob Sømme on the 31st December 1943 to his fellow prisoners at Grini.

'Dear Friends!

There will be no dinner table or speeches tonight. Nor will there be any toasts for the New Year. Still, I would like to stop for a moment on this occasion. It is natural to look backwards, and see what the old year has brought, and forwards to see what hopes and expectations the New Year will bring.

At this time last year, we were told that the enormous progress of the enemy had been stopped and an important turning point had been reached. During the last year we have seen a number of great events. Above all, our eyes have turned against the east where the Russians through several successful battles, have conquered, as far as I remember, an area between three and four times the size of Norway with the most populated and valuable districts of Russia.

The victories from El Alamein to Rome are some of the greatest events. From an Africa cleared of the enemy, the effect across the ocean has been the capitulation of Italy, one of the three enemy nations. The victory against the submarines is another result. Maybe this has made an invasion of the continent possible, and then a fast end to the war. Without doubt, the results that have been achieved during the past year are of vital importance, and by now there is only one possible end to the war. As far as we know, the war may end any day. But in spite of the military results, and in spite of the bombing, the enemy continues its fight with bitter energy. With the same diabolical energy by which it, at the beginning of the war, attacked one defenceless country after another, does it at present fight for every square meter of conquered land with diabolical force and without concern for human lives and material values.

My intention is not to predict what will happen during the year ahead of us. It appears that the end may be quite close. On the other hand, it also appears that fights of long duration will continue for some time. But at least it is impossible to imagine that we will spend yet another year in prison. It seems safe to assume that the year ahead of us will be a year of peace. We must make it our primary wish for the New Year that it will be a year of peace, and not only as after the previous world war, a cease-fire between two catastrophes. Let it be our highest wish that this is the last war in the world's history, and let us not think of this as a Utopian idea or a goal that may never be reached. On the contrary, I believe that this is a goal within the limits of possibility, and much closer than most of us can imagine. In spite of the fact that the catastrophe goes on, I believe that we will win over the war mentality. We must remember that the Allied forces that are fighting against those who started the war represent the largest and most densely populated nations. None of them were armed with the idea of conquering other nations, and this is true for a majority of nations. Remember also the development in our own country, remember the Vikings and the fighting with knives in the villages only a few hundred years ago. Think of the pirates of the last century. By now, the ideas have changed and a peaceful mentality has arrived. There are many signs to show that something between the nations will change and it is probably only a matter of time before peaceful organization and culture will replace the brutality and fanatic vandalism that reigns at present. There is not much we can do for the sake of peace in the coming year. Others will have to draw up the main directions for future peace work. We must remember that everybody is waiting for the peace, and this will demand great obligations from each of us. As Norwegians we are proud and happy that our small country is a nation that participates in the cultural development of the world. But we will be faced with a difficult situation in the year ahead. It is natural that we react against all the cruelty and brutality that we constantly see around us. We would not believe the inhuman treatment of Norwegian prisoners, unless we had the opportunity to witness it almost every day. We have to think about what we shall do when the roles change. It will be natural to discuss the penalties of those Norwegians that have joined the enemy, and who have taken advantage of the situation for their own good. But these thoughts must not be our main concern and directions when the peace arrives. In that case we would have seen that the enemy has been beaten, but also that its diabolical spirit has won. Out task will be to direct the persons that by now are practicing their brutality, and make them and their descendents useful citizens in our future peaceful society. The amount of hate, violence and brutality that the enemy has created all over the world must be eliminated and give room for the spirit of peace and for confidence, trust and understanding among humans. This is the cause for which we have fought and suffered.

I would like to say that this was my personal and greatest goal of my illegal work before I was arrested. The awareness of this has helped me through the long time of imprisonment, and perhaps made these years some of my most valuable and richest. Let this be our hope and our wish for the New Year, that it will be a true year of peace, and let this be the goal for those of us that have experienced and suffered most. This is my personal prayer to all of you, if this should be the last New Year eve in my life. Let us join all our forces for the true sake of peace. Whether you are a farmer from the world's most northerly agriculture, whether you are a fisherman from the uttermost islands on the coast, or an officer from our southern areas, let the sake of peace be the seed we plant when we sometime again will be spread out along our wide stretched country.

Dear friends! Let us look forward to the New Year in a sincere wish for true peace, let us wish each other a happy new and peaceful year.'